Occupy The Solution
not Wall Street

OCCUPY THE SOLUTION NOT WALL STREET

Managing Systemic Bad Debt
with System Gap Theory

Hema Senanayake

authorHOUSE®

AuthorHouse™
1663 Liberty Drive
Bloomington, IN 47403
www.authorhouse.com
Phone: 1-800-839-8640

© 2012 by Hema Senanayake. All rights reserved.

Except for the quotation of short passages for the purposes of criticism and review, no part of this book may be reproduced, stored in a retrieval system, or transmitted by any means without the written permission of the author.

Published by AuthorHouse   08/12/2012

ISBN: 978-1-4772-5698-5 (sc)
ISBN: 978-1-4772-5647-3 (hc)
ISBN: 978-1-4772-5648-0 (e)

Library of Congress Control Number: 2012914192

Any people depicted in stock imagery provided by Thinkstock are models, and such images are being used for illustrative purposes only.
Certain stock imagery © Thinkstock.

This book is printed on acid-free paper.

Because of the dynamic nature of the Internet, any web addresses or links contained in this book may have changed since publication and may no longer be valid. The views expressed in this work are solely those of the author and do not necessarily reflect the views of the publisher, and the publisher hereby disclaims any responsibility for them.

This book is lovingly dedicated to my daughter, Dinushi Vidyanga.

"A dedication is meant to be a permanent memorial."
—*The Guardian*

Private banking assets tend to become public problems in a crisis. By that measure, European countries are far worse off than the US

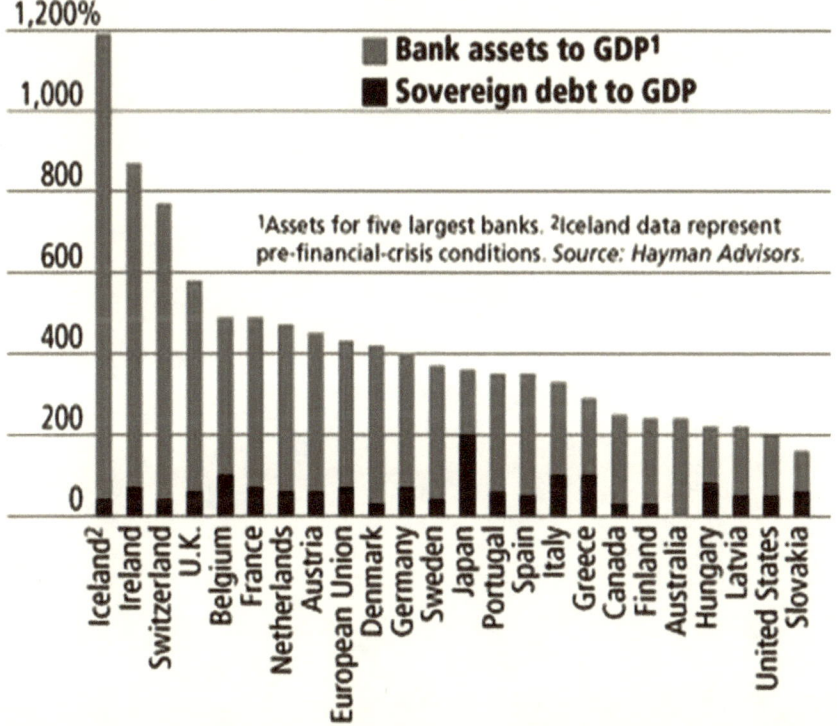

(Courtesy of *Forbes*; February 8, 2010, Volume 185, Number 2, "The Global Debt Bomb.")

Contents

Acknowledgments xi
Introduction 1

Part 1
Theoretical Setting

Chapter 1: Understanding the Functioning of Macroeconomic System Through the Great Recession of 2008 19
Chapter 2: Fractional Reserve Banking System and Full Reserve (or 100 Percent Reserve) Banking 37
Chapter 3: System Gap Theory 51
Chapter 4: The Two-Tier Production System 61
Chapter 5: Market Mechanism and Monetary Mechanism 71
Chapter 6: Achieving Economic Equilibriums or Filling the System Gap 81

Part 2
Analysis of Some Policy Issues and the Solution

Chapter 7: Resolving Some Economic Policy Issues 93
Chapter 8: The Solution 105
Chapter 9: The Question of Pension Planning 119
Chapter 10: Conclusive Remarks 125

Paradigm Shift and Kalama Sutta 129
References 131

Acknowledgments

"Gratitude unlocks the fullness of life."
—Melody Beattie

This book would not be possible without the support and inspiration of numerous people. Since the publication of my first book *Indispensable Bad Debt* in 2008, many people helped shape my views and have inspired me to write this second book. I must thank every one of them.

Yet, without any offense to others, I single out a few. I mostly benefited from Ajith Collonne, Professor Kumar David, Dr. Suren Batagoda, and Professor Piyasena Abeygunawardena; I extend my sincere gratitude to them. Also, I must admit that I benefitted from my merciless critic of Austrian School of economics, Dr. Krassimir Petrove; I extend my sincere gratitude to him too.

What I wrote is an economics book. I am not sure why my father, Sampson, (ninety-four), my mother, Ghana (eighty-six), and my father-in-law, Herbert Mendis (eighty-four) are still fascinated by seeing me involved in literary work. Those seniors have always had a hidden but powerful string of inspiration on the younger generation. I owe them. My eldest brother Kelly is an unbelievably curious man for new ideas who insisted I publish the book sooner; I sincerely thank him.

A special thanks goes to Thalif Deen, Inter Press Service Regional Director—North America and my friends in New York who patiently listened to me and asked valuable questions when I made a point in regard to my subject that was often different from their disciplines. I am thankful to the staff of the publisher of this book, AuthorHouse, for their kind corporation.

My final expression of gratitude goes to my wife, Sheeva, whose love, support, and inspiration never seem to end.

Introduction

"If you can't explain quantum mechanics to a barmaid, then you yourself do not understand it." This is a quote attributed to the great physicist Werner Heisenberg who won the Noble Prize in 1932 for his uncertainty principle. Quantum theory in physics is the most complex and advanced branch of physics; and this was the case especially when Heisenberg worked on it. Yet Heisenberg's view was that you can simplify any profound subject if you really understood it.

This is equally true in economics. If you understand economics, you can simplify it and explain it to the average person. In fact, this is more important in economics than in the physical sciences because, when people vote, they look to the ability of national level political leaders to navigate the economic environment, considering the "economy" directly impacts the well-being of individuals. Therefore, I took great care to explain the difficult economic concepts and theories that are relevant to the topic of this book—as simply as possible.

The modern economic system seems complex. There are a number of theories and schools of economic thought that try to explain the system, how it works, why it fails, and what corrective measures should be taken. Among them, Keynesianism, monetarism, Chicago School of economics, Austrian School of economics, and their variants are prominent. Apart from that, there are many hypotheses and mathematical models, such as Efficient Market Hypothesis (EMH), Rational Expectation Theory (REH), and Dynamic Stochastic General Economic Equilibrium (DSGEE), that are not much discussed in the public domain—but are well known among economists. After the Great Recession of 2008, Hyman Minsky's Financial Instability Hypothesis was rediscovered in an effort to understand the financial crashes. Apart from these theories and concepts of scholars in the capitalist camp, Karl

Marx's thesis of falling rate of profit was re-examined to understand the great economic crash of 2008.

I would suggest the reader forget all the above theories until he or she understands the three economic concepts explained in this book: (1) Mechanics of Recessions (2) Fractional Reserve Banking System, and (3) System Gap Theory. I am strongly convinced that these three concepts will explain the essential, integral parts of the macroeconomic system as a whole. Once you understand these three concepts, you will have an almost perfect understanding of the economic system in which we live today.

Therefore, as the physicist Heisenberg said, the challenge for me is to explain these three concepts as simply as possible in order to be understood by any curious person. If I can't, then I do not know what I am talking about.

I wrote chapter 1 with the above in mind. I have included a small background story in which I explain how I achieved my goal of simplification of theories. At the end of this chapter, I hope you will have a fairly good understanding of these three economic concepts.

Yet, simple versions of economic concepts would not be sufficient to analytical minds. Therefore, Chapter 2 and Chapter 3 are dedicated to explaining the Fractional Reserve Banking System and the System Gap Theory, respectively. Further explanation of Mechanics of Recessions is avoided since this concept is generally agreed upon by all economists.

Once you understand these three concepts, you are requested to understand the next important concept; the "Two-Tier Production System" is explained in Chapter 4.

In order to further strengthen our macroeconomic know-how, I designed chapters 5 and 6. Chapter 5 explains the distinctive roles played by market mechanism and monetary mechanism. Chapter 6 will explain three mechanisms that put the demand-and-supply equilibrium at total output level.

Thereafter, you are almost ready to understand and discuss any economic policy issue that matters to you, your country, and the world. Some of those economic policy issues could be about the austerity measures, increasing deficit financing of the government to resolve economic crises, or trade imbalances. Some policy issues could be about monetary system issues, taxation, or fair distribution of distributable output. Whatever the macroeconomic issue, you will have an enlightened view after understanding the fundamental concepts explained in the first part of the book: the Theoretical Setting.

In order to complete the theoretical setting of the book, I wanted to write on the theory of pension planning as the last chapter of the theoretical part. For a reason that you may find later, I wanted to treat the subject of pension planning as a macroeconomic subject. I purposely moved it to after we discuss a solution to prevent crashing the macroeconomic system and how we can fix it rather quickly if it does crash.

In Chapter 7, we discuss some selective policy issues with the use of theoretical understanding gained in preceding chapters.

System Gap Theory (SGT) establishes that the present capitalist economic system is not in natural equilibrium; instead, it has an inherent systemic contradiction. As a result, the economic system behaves in a unique way. This behavior could be summarized as follows:

After a period of economic growth, if the private consumers are not in significant debt, then the government should be. And if both the private consumer and the government are not in debt significantly, then the System Gap must be filling from the income derived from the stock and derivative market, which means there should be a bubble in the stock market with heavy debt on holders or holding companies of stocks and derivatives.

If none of the above is happening, then it must be an immature economy that is expanding by reinvesting the expanded capital and producer credit—mostly producing goods and services that do not satisfy the demand of immediate consumption. In all former scenarios—except the last scenario—the economic system should crash sooner than later due to heavy debt, if partial debt cancellation does not take place proactively. In the latter case, the economy would fall into any one of the former scenarios as the economy grows. The only other possibility where a producer country does not have a "debt" crisis is when it continues to have an excessive trade surplus, but all countries in the world cannot record excessive trade surpluses.

Any system is subjected to the "cause-and-effect" principle. Since it is a universal principle, what I explain above must be the effect of certain underlying causes. However, when the cause is in motion, the effect is unavoidable. If we want to change the effect, we have to change the underlying cause.

SGT accurately explains the underlying cause of the above effect. Once the cause is known, then only you can make an attempt to change the cause and stop the effect. From the theory of gravity, we know why things are pulled toward the earth. That means we know the cause. Scientists set the opposite causes to shoot a satellite to space. Likewise, the economy—under present macroeconomic practice—moves toward a systemic crash after a period of growth. Therefore, economists need to change the causes at the appropriate time to prevent such crashes. That's the only solution.

The solution to the systemic debt crises is discussed in detail in Chapter 8 under the title "The Solution." As I mentioned earlier I want to discuss the subject of pension planning after we discuss a solution to prevent crashing the macroeconomic system. So, Chapter 9 is about pension planning. Chapter 10 will have some important conclusive remarks. Now you have a good outline of this book.

"The problem is not the ignorance but the illusion of knowledge."
—Professor Daniel J Boorstin

Part 1
Theoretical Setting

Chapter 1
Understanding the Functioning of Macroeconomic System through the Great Recession of 2008

The economic system has to be fixed; this notion is now unanimous around the world after the Great Recession of 2008. You can't fix a system if you do not understand it or if you do not understand how it works as a whole.

Sometimes events and occurrences reveal how a system really works. Likewise, the Great Recession of 2008 (which is sometimes referred to as the great crash of 2008) reveals the inner workings of the modern "complex" economic system.

In 2008, the world's wealthiest nation, the United States, suddenly revealed to the world that the US economic system and the society had accumulated enormous debt and other monetary obligations that could not be paid back or honored. The incumbent president, Barack Obama, said "I think it is important to understand that some of that wealth was illusionary in the first place." ("After the Great Recession" interview with President Obama, *New York Times Magazine*, April 28, 2009)

Without the occurrence of the Great Crash of 2008, such contradiction of wealth and bad debt would not have surfaced. What is important is that such contradictions would continue—and the same occurrences will take place if we do not fix the system. Understanding this systemic contradiction is the first step in fixing the problem.

Therefore, I will use the systemic crash of 2008 to explain the inner workings of the contemporary economic system. Yet, my primary objective in this chapter is not to explain the events of 2008; instead, I want to introduce three economic concepts to the reader that will facilitate understanding how the modern macroeconomic system works. This knowledge will lead to understanding the systemic contradiction that we have to deal with.

Those three economic concepts are (1) Mechanics of Recessions (2) Fractional Reserve Banking System, and (3) System Gap Theory. These three concepts explain the fundamental and integral parts of the macroeconomic system. Without knowing these concepts accurately, no one could understand the economic system as a whole or understand the true reasons behind the crash of 2008. They also couldn't figure out the true solutions rather than increasing the deficit financing of the government on public projects and programs as done in the US or suggesting austerity measures as done in Europe.

The important thing is that you do not need to be an economist to understand these concepts. Any curious reader will understand them without any difficulty in this chapter since I took great care to simplify them. Let me explain them with a small background story through which you may find how I achieved the goal of simplification of theories/concepts.

I was invited to deliver a public lecture on February 10, 2012, on the topic of the "Global Economic Crisis of 2008—Reasons and Solutions." This crisis was something I wrote articles about and I duly claim that I predicted it. The challenge was that I had to do it in thirty minutes. The organizers had allocated thirty minutes for the initial monologue presentation and two hours or more to discuss questions. The logic behind their time allocation was simple. They were of the opinion that the attention of most participants in public lectures is good for the first thirty minutes. If I could arouse their attention and establish my main points in first thirty minutes of my presentation, the rest of the time would be used effectively in answering questions. Their rationale was sensible, and I agreed to do the seminar. I had a fear about the time limit because it was a subject discussed in volumes and volumes of books.

As you may know, the Global Economic Crisis of 2008 became very serious and complex. The European Commission at one point totally rejected the existing macroeconomic theories as incapable of predicting crises and also was incapable of giving any insight to resolve the crises. Many economic scholars have been disappointed by the way things have turned around. Yet many economic scholars, Central Bankers, and policymakers submitted their own theories and views, which did not find consensus as of today. Arguments among Keynesians, monetarists, economists of Chicago School, and economists of Austrian School seem to never end. Apart from that, presidents and prime ministers of troubled countries, IMF, the World Bank, and the International Bank of Settlements (IBS) had their own "pragmatic" explanations. On the other side of the spectrum, there are Marxist scholars who revived Marx's thesis of "falling rate of profit" to explain the crisis, which could not be simply ignored.

But my goal was not to present any existing idea or another controversial view. My goal was to achieve a consensus. Yet in an environment of diverse opinions and views, how a person can explain the crisis of 2008 in thirty minutes with an objective to achieve a consensus of a crisis that is still continuing after nearly four years. However, in this environment, if somebody could achieve a consensus, then he must be presenting a provable truth.

In November 2008, I published a new macro-economic theory called "The Theory of Economic System Gap" in *Indispensable Bad Debt* to explain the world economic crisis. I knew I had some strong arguments on the subject. Most of those who did read that book never rejected the theory or main arguments presented there. Along with that theory and two other fundamental economic and financial concepts—Mechanics of Recessions and Fractional Reserve Banking—I knew I could present a good case. I was confident that I would achieve my goal but allocated time for the initial presentation was still a challenge.

The economic system itself is a complex one—at least it seems so for many people. It is not a simple production economy anymore, but it has enormously large financial market too. In order to provide a reasonable insight, it is highly required to provide a reasonable understanding of the macroeconomic system. Moreover, the core banking system, through which the modern economy is powered, is itself a complex one called Fractional Reserve Banking. Again System Gap Theory requires a good amount of time to understand it properly. I knew I would not achieve my goal of obtaining a consensus from the audience if I did not explain or touch these aspects properly. How it could be done in thirty minutes?

Then I realized that simplification was the only solution. Without simplifying these economic concepts, I would not be able to achieve my goal.

This was a situation where anybody could be influenced by the words of Werner Heisenberg, the great physicist. Werner Heisenberg contributed to the subject of quantum theory immensely. Once he said that if you can't explain quantum mechanics to a barmaid (a lady who sells beer in pubs/restaurants), then you yourself do not know about it. The message of his idea is that "simplification" is what is most important in profound subjects. But simplification would not devalue the profoundness of the subjects that need to be discussed.

Similar thoughts struck in my mind—and then I began to write my presentation. I wanted to do it as a PowerPoint presentation. I started to prepare slides too. Initially, the number of slides came to twenty-two. My wife laughed at me, saying that I could not use twenty-two slides for a thirty-minute presentation. Then I gave my notes for the speech to her and asked her to prepare the slides. She made a lot of changes, but the number of slides remained the same.

But that exercise did help me a lot. She is a laywoman when comes to economics. By profession, she is a computer systems analyst. From the slides she prepared, I understood the way that any lay intellectual or any curious listener would understand this difficult subject. I used her slides to redraft my speech. Thanks to her effort, the necessary simplification I had been looking for was achieved. Then I realized I did not need any slides to deliver the lecture.

I gave up the idea of making a PowerPoint presentation. I did the presentation on the scheduled date within the allocated time for a small but diverse crowd. Immediately after the lecture, I realized to a greater extent that I was going to achieve a consensus for my explanation on what we identify now as the Great Recession of 2008. The question-and-answer session went almost two and a half hours. The audience was satisfied.

I strongly felt that I achieved my goal of achieving consensus and so did the organizers because they achieved their goal of organizing a good public lecture.

I submit below extracts of the lecture notes I used in that seminar. It is a good start to dig into this controversial subject.

(1) Mechanics of Recession

Let us assume that a producer produces a consumable item. He expects consumers to buy what he offered to the market. If consumers did not buy, the producer cuts back his volume of production, which leads to a recession because reduction of output is defined as a recession.

Economic system produces two kinds of commodities.

1) Commodities for consumption.
2) Commodities for the use of production i.e. capital goods.

Total output consists of these two kinds of commodities.

Capital goods are in demand only to produce consumables. If the production of commodities for consumption is reduced, the demand for capital goods will be reduced. As a result, total output will be reduced. If total output is reduced for two consecutive quarters, it is officially defined as a recession by economists.

Recessions cannot occur in contemporary economic systems outside the above mechanisms if we ignore the reduction of output due to natural disasters. Hence the above explains the mechanics of recessions.

(2) Fractional Reserve Banking System

This is the second concept we need to understand accurately.

If I give you $100 and ask you to lend it, how much can you lend? According to common sense, you cannot lend more than $100 because that is the sum of money you have.

But under the Fractional Reserve System, you can lend $900 or so out of a deposit of $100. This is the core banking practice in the contemporary economic system. You have to understand the concept of Fractional Reserve Banking System accurately because most explanations—even in many scholarly books and on the Internet—are not accurate.

It is believed that this practice was started in middle centuries by goldsmiths. People used to keep their extra gold/silver with the goldsmiths for safekeeping. He issued a note from his notebook for each deposit. Sometimes people also came to goldsmith to borrow gold deposited by others.

Let us assume that people deposited 100 gold coins. He issued one note for each gold coin. So, depositors had 100 notes. The goldsmith returned anybody's gold upon the submission of notes. The goldsmith observed that only 10 percent of notes were submitted to withdraw their gold at any particular time. Subsequently what was withdrawn was usually deposited back. Firstly, the goldsmith thought he could lend ninety gold coins out of a deposit of 100 coins because only 10 percent is withdrawn at any given time. So, he lent only ninety coins out of the 100.

Secondly, the goldsmith thought he would issue a note to any borrower instead of real gold. People liked it because they believed that goldsmith would pay back actual gold upon submission of notes. Now assume that the goldsmith has 100 coins in deposits. He issues 100 notes to depositors. Also he decides to issue 900 notes to borrowers; each note has a value of one gold coin.

Now, there are 1,000 notes in circulation: 100 notes with depositors and 900 notes with borrowers. His past experience says that 10 percent of notes would be submitted to him at any given time to withdraw actual gold coins.

So, 10 percent of 1,000 is 100; this means the goldsmith is supposed to have 100 actual gold coins in reserve to honor any possible withdrawal if he puts 1,000 notes into circulation.

He has 100 coins in reserve because he did not issue gold coins to any borrower. Therefore, the goldsmith did not face any problem—even if he lent 900 out of an incoming deposit of 100 gold coins. This is a mechanism to create more credit out of a relatively lesser amount of incoming deposit.

In this system, the goldsmith issued 1,000 notes. He is liable to issue one gold coin for each note. So, his total liability is 1,000. He kept only 100 gold coins in reserve. This means the system has a fraction of actual cash reserves to total liability. That is why it is called Fractional Reserve Banking.

Fractional Reserve System is the modern banking practice done through commercial banks with the full backing of the Federal Reserve or the Central Bank.

But this Fractional Reserve System is inherently bankrupt. If 20 percent of notes (i.e. 200) were submitted to withdraw actual gold (cash) the goldsmith can't pay. He is virtually bankrupt because he had only 100 coins. In that event, the goldsmith can temporarily borrow from another goldsmith—it is a situation of a lender borrowing from another lender. In modern days, this practice is in use and is called interbank borrowing. This means in order to sustain the banking system, bank-to-bank lending is crucially important.

If all goldsmiths face the same problem, then the system needs an "ultimate lender." In modern days, the ultimate lender is the Central Bank. In 2008, American Central Bank (Federal Reserve) saved all major banks. It was like a situation when 20 percent of notes came to the goldsmith. The best example is the collapse of IndyMac in July 2008. However big or good the banking system appears to be, it is an inherently fragile system under the Fractional Reserve System. Why do we need this fragile system? Keep this question in mind, but let us go to the final concept called "System Gap Theory."

(3) System Gap Theory

In the present economic system, a producer sells his product to a consumer, another entrepreneur, or both parties. This system is called an un-integrated economic system. Instead of this system, let us take a simple production economy to understand the System Gap Theory. You may find later that this theory equally applies to any un-integrated system with or without large financial markets.

In our simple economy, a producer does not sell to another entrepreneur. He should sell only to consumers. Also in this simple system, the producer does not invest money to buy from another producer because there is no buying and selling among producers. So, he should invest only on labor. In economics, this system is called a "Fully Integrated Economic System."

Now let us consider that a producer invests $500 to produce something. As he does not buy anything from another producer, that $500 must be spent on labor. What is paid for labor is the income of consumers. So consumer income is $500 in this system; this obviously includes the remuneration earned by the entrepreneur for his consumption.

Thinking that it is required to have a capital reserve to expand the business, the entrepreneur values his product at $590. That is the sum of money that the entrepreneur expects from consumers. Now the value of consumables offered is $590, and the consumer income is $500. So, there is a gap between the value of consumables offered and the consumer income (which is a lesser amount). This gap is the

System Gap when the values represent the sum of total sales proceeds and the sum of total consumer income.

So, the System Gap Theory explains that the economic system can never pay consumers an aggregate income that equals or exceeds the value of consumables offered by the system. The contemporary economic system is not a simple production economy, but it has a large financial market. We will bring it up later in this discussion. (Please note that the existence of the System Gap for the modern economic system has been proved—and that document was distributed during the lecture. The same with a little more detail is presented in the Chapter 3 of this book).

Yet, if the consumer did not buy what is offered, then the producer cut back production. That is how a recession starts. We learned about it above from the Mechanics of Recessions.

So, the consumer must spend $590 to put the economic system into equilibrium or, in other words, to have demand-and-supply equilibrium. How do the consumers spend $590 while having an income of $500? This is how it happens.

Some consumers save a little bit of money. Let us assume they save $100 collectively. This money can be loaned to another consumer. So, now consumers spend $400—plus a loan of $100. Still the total is $500 and $90 is short, and the system is not in equilibrium. This means if we have a banking system that creates loans subjected to the limits of savings, the system will be in disequilibrium.

But if we can create credit amounting to $190 based on the saving of $100, then the system will be in equilibrium. Then we should have a banking system to create more credit based on a little savings in order to ensure that producers would get back what they expect from consumers.

We just learned such a banking system under Fractional Reserve Banking. It is the Fractional Reserve System that puts the system into equilibrium while filling the System Gap in the medium to long term.

That's the reason we need to have the Fractional Reserve Banking system—however fragile that system is. Therefore we must stabilize the Fractional Reserve System through some other measure, but we cannot afford to do without it. (Austrian School economists propose to eliminate the Fractional Reserve System.)

However, the story does not end there. In this system, the income is $500. But they consumed something to the value of $590. If a family spends beyond its income, it accumulates debt in each month. After a while, they have debt that cannot be paid back. Lenders do not lend anymore.

If lenders do not lend, then the System Gap is not filled—and the producer does not get what he expects from consumers. If producers do not get back what they expect from consumers, they cut back production, which would reduce the total output and then recession begins.

Is this how the world recession began in late 2007?

The answer is yes. The financial crash was rooted in the failure of consumer credit mechanism. Until we consider the role of the financial sector, let us consider the role played by the private consumer debt.

- German consumer lenders reported that the consumer loan market was saturated in 2006—one year prior to the crash.
- France said consumer loan market was near saturation in 2006.
- In the UK, debt collectors reported that its agents had contacted 17 million people in 2006. Everybody knows why debt collectors contact people.
- In the US, home foreclosures were about to exceed 2 million in 2006.

What the above information tell you?

That information tells you that the consumer credit mechanism was about to fail in 2007. If consumers did not get loans, the System Gap would not be filled. As a result, producers would not get back what they needed from consumer—and a recession should take place. This means you can predict recessions if you know that the filling of the System Gap is going to break.

The conclusion is that the recession in the US and in Europe arose due to "bad debt." Everybody identified that the reason for the crisis was "bad debt." Then they attributed the blame to greediness of lenders and borrowers. Wall Street executives pushed bad loans and—knowingly or unknowingly—American families took them. President Obama said, "This financial crisis wasn't just the result of decisions made in the executive suites on Wall Street; it was also the result of decisions made around kitchen tables across America, by folks taking on mortgages and credit cards and auto loans. And while it's true that many Americans took on financial obligations they knew—or should have known—they could not afford, millions of others were, frankly, duped. They were misled by deceptive terms and conditions, buried deep in the fine print." (President Barack Obama, Cooper Union address, April, 2010)

But none saw that accumulation of bad debt arose as a result of a contradiction in the macroeconomic system that required creating a component of bad debt in the system in filling of the System Gap with credit.

Let us now bring the role of "financial market" into this discussion.

In our former example, consumers saved $100. As a result, the system has to create consumer credit amounting to $190 to put the system into equilibrium.

In stock markets, people derive a certain income for the use of consumption when stock prices are increasing. Now we have $100 in savings. Let us put that in the stock market to derive a certain amount of income for the use of consumption. The quantum of money needed for consumption through the appreciation of stocks is $190, so that the system would be in equilibrium.

Let us assume stocks are appreciating at 50 percent. If $190 equals 50 percent of market capitalization after stock appreciation, then we will have $190 to fill the System Gap. So, we can calculate the value for initial market capitalization. It is $380. Now 50 percent appreciation of $380 is $190. We can use this $190 for consumption, and the system is in equilibrium.

Within the figure of $380, we have $100 invested from savings. Where did the balance come from? It came from credit created by the Fractional Reserve System. The debt component of market capitalization is $290 (380-100). Yet what is capitalized in the stock market is called financial assets.

If we give direct consumer credit, the system has debt of $190 when the system is in equilibrium. Under stock market capitalization, the system has debt of $290 at initial market capitalization when the system is in equilibrium.

What does this mean?

- Stock market capitalization is not purely a saving-based process; part of it is debt-based.
- Stock markets might carry more debt than consumer debt.
- If stock markets collapse, defaults would be more.
- When consumers default, it becomes "bad debt"
- When stock markets default, it becomes "toxic assets."

In view of above discussion, now you are ready to fully understand the reasons for the global economic crisis that erupted in late 2007 in the United States and Europe. Let us list the sequence of events:

1. Consumers, including homeowners, were in heavy debt.
2. Consumer defaults increased.
3. European fund providers stopped funds (fairly smaller amounts) to the American housing market (at the beginning of August 2007)
4. Filling of System Gap began to break. Demand for houses reduced.

5. Housing-related stocks plunged and defaults increased in the stock market.
6. Commercial banks' inflows from loan repayments went haywire. Their daily balancing act became difficult without new deposits or new capital.
7. People suspected the stability of banks.
8. People began to withdraw deposits. (It was like a situation that 20 percent notes came to the goldsmith). In the United States, the FDIC tried to stop withdrawals by undertaking to guarantee the payment of almost all deposits if a bank fails.
9. All major banks (including too-big-to-fail banks) were in bankruptcy or liquidity crisis.
10. Share prices of financial institutions came down, increasing more defaults.
10. Since banks were in crisis, the credit mechanism further shrank.
11. Failure of System Gap went to a new height.
12. Producers cut back jobs. Consumer income further came down.
13. When consumer income is low (from stocks and loss of jobs), the failure of System Gap continued.
14. By the end of 2008, it was full-blown economic crisis in the US and Europe; difficulties spread around the world.

Accordingly in view of above discussion, what is the first conclusion we can make? The first conclusion is that the economic system cannot grow if consumers did live within their means, which is also the main reason for arising systemic bad debt. This is not to suggest extreme consumerism is good; instead the proposition is under extreme consumerism or under frugal level of consumption, the economic system has to live beyond its debt-free monetary income. This is the contradiction we have in our production system.

I concluded my monologue presentation at this point. I realized that participants were appreciative of the simplification of economic theories and concepts—and the way I combined them to give an insight as to how the macroeconomic system works and fails.

Solutions were discussed in the question-and-answer session. Below are some excerpts. But the solution to this contradiction and to resolve the ongoing global economic crisis has been discussed in detail in Chapter 8 of this book.

1) Our macroeconomic system is not in natural equilibrium. Our economic system is such that it requires that the system must live beyond its means (or beyond the allocated consumable income). The requirement to consume beyond the income arises due to a systemic contradiction pointed out by System Gap Theory. Such consumption is temporarily facilitated by creation of a component of bad debt and such bad debt is camouflaged (1) in consumer debt, (2) in the debt created in the stock and derivative markets, and (3) in the government debt accumulated through deficit financing, but those bad debts would surface during an economic crash, which crashes are inevitable under the known application of economic policies.

2) Due to the existence of System Gap after a certain period of economic growth, if private consumers are not in significant debt, then the government should be. And if both the private consumer and the government are not in debt significantly, then the System Gap must be filling from the income derived from the stock market, which means there should be a bubble in the stock market with heavy debt on holders or holding companies of stocks. If none of the above is happening, it must be an immature economy, which is expanding by reinvesting the expanded capital and producer credit. In all former scenarios except the last scenario, the economic system should crash sooner than later if systemic debt cancellation does not take place proactively. In the latter case, the economy would fall into any one of the former scenarios as the economy grows. The only other possibility that a producer country does not have a debt crisis is that it continues to have excessive trade surplus, but all countries in the world cannot record trade surpluses.

3) Keynes believed that continuing investments would bring economic equilibrium. But it is only a temporary mechanism. (This point has been discussed in Chapter 3). In other words, continuing

investment in a real economy is not a mechanism to have the demand-and-supply equilibrium in the long run. Then if we are not greatly interested in creating credit in the stock market to make bubbles to enable to fill the System Gap, we are left with only one alternative to fill the System Gap—that is to revive the consumer credit mechanism.

Therefore it is an unavoidable necessity for the economic system to create consumer credit beyond their collective savings in order to ensure that producers get back what they expect from consumers out of their expenditure, putting the economic system into equilibrium. This contributes to the capital accumulation process.

Accumulation of capital and its investment further increases consumer income so that more lending to consumers becomes possible.

But, since we create consumer credit beyond their savings, the system should accumulate a non-repayable amount of debt. This reflects the increasing consumer debt-to-income ratio. At a certain point—due to the staggering amount of debt—either the consumer cannot borrow as they did in the past or lenders are not willing to lend to consumers. At this point, the economic System Gap would not be filled at the existing output level. When this happens, a recession is unavoidable; a recession creates job slumps and income fears.

If this process did not take place in the consumer regime, the debt creation process should have taken place in deficit financing of the government or in financial markets leading to a boom. Booms cannot last forever.

4) This systemic behavior is common to any money-based system—no matter if the system is capitalist or socialist or any other. Crashes can be prevented proactively by a general cancellation of part of the debt. Accordingly, the creation of consumer credit beyond their collective savings and the subsequent part cancellation of bad debt contribute to sustaining the economic growth. Modern economic

practice lacks this second part so that periodic systemic crashes occur. Some people might think that periodic part cancellation of debt might lead to a moral hazard, but moral hazards occur when case-by-case bankruptcies are allowed—not by the general debt deflation by policy actions. (In this book, we will take up this point in Chapter 8).

The only moral question is whether we should allow stock and derivative markets to create so much bad debt in the economic system.

Because the severity of crashes are heavily compounded by the fact that how many stocks and their derivatives are credit financed by commercial banks because when the consumer "debt" crises surface, the value of stocks plummeted, making the financial assets sour. This will create a new liquidity crisis in the banks, virtually stopping issuing credits which contributes to the continuing failure of the filling of the System Gap.

5) Some economists, including Nobel laureates, suggest that global trade imbalance is a reason for the crash of economies in the US and in Europe. If trade deficit caused this crisis, then why did Japan, which had a continuing trade surplus, hit a crisis in the early 1990s? As usual, its hidden bad debt surfaced with the crisis. The Japanese economy is subjected to the behavior explained by SGT. The trade imbalance did not cause the problem in the US and Europe, but the trade deficit played a role in increasing the gravity of the crisis.

6) In the early twentieth century, people officially and wishfully adopted the system of creating more credit than savings or incoming deposits under Fractional Reserve Banking system. (The US Federal Reserve was created in 1913). Similarly, in the early twenty-first century, people will and should develop macroeconomic (monetary) policies for the general cancellation of part of bad debt (uncollectible debt) proactively before crashes occur. This is imperative for the advancement of civilization.

7) Some economists say that boom-and-bust cycles are a natural phenomenon in the economic system and boom-and-bust cycles have been around for centuries. I pointed out that the development of physical productive forces is not cyclical, but we have a macroeconomic system that follows boom-and-bust cycles. If the development of physical productive power behaves in a boom-and-bust cyclical pattern, we have to tolerate the boom-and-bust cycle of macroeconomic output and the system as a whole. But if the progress of the physical productive power or even the potential of the increment of physical productive power is progressive, it is not necessary for us to tolerate the cyclical behavior of the macroeconomic system. This does not mean that the business cycles of microeconomic systems (which correspond to the performance of individual enterprises) should not be tolerated; instead, such cyclical behavior is necessary to ensure business efficiency that is based on consumer preferences. Businesses should be allowed to fail—and new businesses should be allowed to emerge—based on efficiency and consumer preferences. But macroeconomic systems fail not due to consumer preferences but due to the general illiquidity of consumers arising from a bad debt crisis as explained by System Gap Theory. The illiquidity of consumers is not a physical phenomenon but a monetary phenomenon. Then it is obvious that we could have prevented the collapse of the macroeconomic system in the US and Europe in late 2007—and the continuing crisis could have been resolved rather quickly. But the invention of new macroeconomic policy tool is what was and is needed.

I hope you have a penetrating view of the macroeconomic system. Before I finish this chapter, let me present one of the important ideas suggested by Professor Joseph E. Stiglitz in regard to the resolution of the great crash of 2008. His views are selected because he was a former chief economist of the World Bank and is a Nobel laureate.

He says, "We will now have to reconstruct a society with a better balance between the role of government and the role of the market. More balance can lead to a more efficient and a more stable economy." (*Free Fall,* 2010, p. 185).

According to him, what you need to do is strike a proper balance between the role of government and the role of the market with some micro-level structural adjustments—and there will not be a bad debt crisis that leads to economic crashes. Unfortunately, this is a myth that cannot be defeated because whenever another crisis takes place, you can find fault with the role of the government and the role of the market. The only way to defeat this mythology is to demand an explanation as to whether the contemporary economic system is in natural equilibrium or not. If the system is not in natural equilibrium, we have to do something new instead of striking a "proper" balance between the role of government and the role of market. (Please refer to Chapter 4.) Out of the six key economic challenges he identified that the world faces today, there is none about a systemic contradiction that leads to accumulate bad debt during periods of growth.

Keeping this in mind, let us strengthen our knowledge in the following chapters until we discuss a solution to the contradictions in the macroeconomic system.

Chapter 2
Fractional Reserve Banking System and Full Reserve (or 100 Percent Reserve) Banking

From Chapter 1, we know that Fractional Reserve Banking is a system that could lend $900 or so out of an incoming deposit of $100. In short, it is a system that could create more credit out of a fairly small incoming deposit. Let us discuss it further—along with Full Reserve Banking system—in order to gain an in-depth understanding of one of the most important parts of the macroeconomic system.

The difference between the two systems, at a glance, is that under the Fractional Reserve system, the commercial banks can create "money (in fact, monetary substitute)" and under the Full Reserve Banking system, commercial banks cannot create money.

So, at least there are two kinds of banking systems that we should be concerned with: Full Reserve Banking system and the Fractional Reserve Banking system. The system we practice today is Fractional Reserve Banking. A large group of economists who drafted the American Monetary Reform Act suggest doing away with Fractional Reserve System and establishing Full Reserve Banking system. These economists officially claim that Milton Friedman of the Chicago School of Economics, in his later years supported (sympathized) this proposal. (http://www.themoneymasters.com/monetary-reform-act/principles-of-monetary-reform/). But most Central Bankers prefer the Fractional Reserve system.

In a democratic society, people have the capability to choose one system over the other. In fact, Congressman Dr. Ron Paul was successful in creating a considerable sociopolitical movement to end the Fractional Reserve System together with the Federal Reserve, which is the Central Bank of the US. In a book published in 2010, he said, "Today there is a growing social movement, even a political movement, dedicated to ending the Fed." (Ron Paul, *End the Fed*, p. 4). If this movement of Ron Paul becomes a mass movement, then possibly through a democratic process, the United States would end the Fractional Reserve Banking system—the system that allows commercial banks to create money.

In fact, which system do we need? This question is important because modern civilizations are based on a money system. Bad money systems can destroy civilizations. That is why everybody should care about this subject.

I think there is a consensual basis to resolve this question. There are certain things called macroeconomic fundamentals. If macroeconomic fundamentals demand a certain system, we have to use that system. If the macroeconomic system does not require any particular system, then the choice between two systems is political. First, we need to understand the two systems of banking.

These two banking systems have two distinct differences. One is that under the Fractional Reserve Banking system, most of the money created in a country is done by the designated commercial banks; under the Full Reserve Banking system, this power of commercial banks is removed and the government becomes the sole authority to create money.

Today's Fractional Reserve Banking system can fairly and easily be converted into the Full Reserve Banking system with the following proposal mentioned in the American Monetary Reform Act.

"Sec. 4. ONE HUNDRED PERCENT (100 percent) RESERVE REQUIREMENT. Section 19(b)(2)(A-D) of the Federal Reserve Act is hereby amended to raise the Reserve Requirement ratio for financial institutions, in equal monthly increments of eight and one-half percent

(8.5 percent), to one hundred percent (100 percent)." (http://www.themoneymasters.com/monetary-reform-act/)

Under the above proposal, all banks become complete intermediaries without the ability to create money (or monetary substitutes) within a year since the transition is set to be gradual by the increment of reserve requirement over a few months until 100 percent reserve requirement is reached. So, there is nothing difficult about the conversion of one system to another.

The second distinct difference of these two banking systems is that under the Fractional Reserve system, designated commercial banks can create more credit out of a fairly small incoming deposit. For an example, if the incoming deposit is $100, the bank can literally loan out $900 or so under the existing rules of Fractional Reserve system—while in the Full Reserve system, the bank can lend a maximum of $100. Accordingly, the Fractional Reserve system is a system to create more credit based on a little savings.

If the macroeconomic fundamentals need a banking system that could create more credit out of a little savings, then we must retain the Fractional Reserve system. If the macroeconomic fundamentals do not demand a system that could create more credit out of a little savings, then the Full Reserve system would be best because that system is more stable than the Fractional Reserve system.

Now the question we need to resolve is whether the macroeconomic system needs a banking system that could create more credit out of fairly small incoming cash deposits in order to have economic equilibrium in the system. We discussed it briefly in Chapter 1 and will discuss this question a little deeper in the next chapter.

Before that, we need to understand these two systems clearly. Therefore this chapter is dedicated to discussing the operational aspects of these two banking systems.

The question of the modern banking system, which is a Fractional Reserve System, is still unresolved for many. I found out that what many universities teach in regard to this subject is not accurate. Also, I found out that leading web-based encyclopedias do not explain this peculiar system accurately.

Let us look at a few examples. The quote below is a passage in regard to the Fractional Reserve system explained in *The Nature of Money*. The author is a Cambridge University professor in political economy; his association with Cambridge University has been over a period of forty years. The explanation as he tries to explain the contemporary Fractional Reserve system is completely inaccurate.

"Assuming that a bank operates with a 10 percent Fractional Reserve, for every £100 deposited (liabilities), it is able to advance loans (assets) of £90. As it is spent, this monetized debt appears in bank accounts elsewhere in the system. In turn, further deposits are created against which these other banks may extend loans—in the first instance, a loan of £81 (£90 minus £9 (10 percent of Fractional Reserve) = £81). Eventually, the initial deposit of £100 could produce £900 of new money in the form of loans." (Ingham G., *The Nature of Money*, Polity Press, 2004, p. 139).

Similarly let us take another example. Ben Bernanke is the current chairman of the Federal Reserve of the United States. Carefully study the following quote of Ben Bernanke. He made these remarks on November 21, 2002, before the National Economic Club in Washington:

> The US government has a technology called a printing press (or, today, its electronic equivalent), that allows it to produce as many US dollars as it wishes at essentially no cost. By increasing the number of US dollars in circulation, or even by credibly threatening to do so, the US government can also reduce the value of a dollar in terms of goods and services, which is equivalent to raising the prices in dollars of those goods and services. We conclude that, under a paper-money system, a determined government can always generate higher spending and hence positive inflation. (*End the Fed*; 2010, Ron Paul, pp. 10 and 11)

You may easily find later in this chapter that the above quote does not accurately explain how the money stock in the economic system increases because, without any involvement by the government, the stock of money in circulation can be increased simply by the act of lending by commercial banks and in fact, the creation of "money" by banks is the main mechanism of increasing the money in circulation when we choose Fractional Reserve Banking system, which is the system the United States practices today.

These two examples clearly demand an accurate explanation in regard to the increase of the stock of money under the modern practice of the Fractional Reserve System. However, this process of increasing money stock under Fractional Reserve System has been best explained in the MacMillan Committee Report in 1931. It was a committee on finance and industry of British Parliament. The MacMillan Committee was appointed by a Labour Government in 1929 "to enquire into banking, finance, and credit, paying regard to the factors, both internal and international, which govern their operation, and to make recommendations calculated to enable their agencies to promote the development of trade and commerce and the employment of labour." You may find the relevant quote elsewhere in this chapter.

Economists are divided on the issue of banks' ability to create money. Some economists say banks are just intermediaries—and some say banks are not just intermediaries. Instead, they say that banks create money, which they lend. So, we have two clear differences of opinions.

Apart from that, those who say that banks create money are divided into two schools of thought. One group of economists argues a bank cannot lend more than what they get in deposits, but through the network of banks, ultimately the banking system can create more money than incoming deposits. The other group rejected this notion and argues that one bank can lend more than an incoming cash deposit and such lending creates new money.

So, at least all these economists must be talking about two system of banking. One must be a system where banks cannot lend more than what they are getting in as deposits. In the other system of banking, the

41

system could lend more than what they are getting as deposits—even though the explanation of the process of creating credit differs. The first system is generally known as Full Reserve Banking or 100 Percent Reserve Banking, and the other is known as Fractional Reserve Banking.

Sometimes difficult phenomena could be best explained through stories. Similarly, the following story is useful to understanding the said two concepts easily, quickly, and accurately. Even though part of this story has been mentioned in Chapter 1, the narration of it here in full would not be felt as repetition.

It is believed that in the middle centuries, goldsmiths started the practice of so-called "Fractional Reserve" system. People deposited part of their gold with goldsmiths for safekeeping. The goldsmith then issued a note to the depositor. The goldsmith returned any person's gold on return of his note. Sometimes, he charged a small fee for his service payable by gold or silver.

When people wanted to borrow, they came to goldsmiths. Goldsmiths have deposits of other's gold, and knowing that everybody would not withdraw all the gold deposited at any one time, he could lend gold from the deposits in his custody. Accordingly, the maximum he could loan out was the deposit he had. However, he had to keep a fraction of the deposits as a precautionary measure to return to the depositor whenever a depositor came to withdraw his or her deposit.

Since the note issued on the deposit was honored by the goldsmith, sometimes people used the notes to settle their payments among themselves. Now, the goldsmiths understood that people were not withdrawing their gold at any one time, and his notes were considered as money—the gold—in executing transactions.

Given this understanding, he decided to issue a note when people came to borrow gold to pay their debt or make payment to another. Since the note was exchangeable for gold when it was presented to the goldsmith, people liked it. It was easy to carry and handle too.

A goldsmith's note was just a piece of paper. He could create any amount of them. So, he could lend any amount to borrowers in the form of notes. However, there were certain limits.

Let us consider two examples (or two scenarios) to understand it.

1st Example (scenario one)

People deposited 100 gold coins. So, the goldsmith issued notes to the value of 100. At the remotest possibility, sometimes they withdrew 10 percent of it, which meant 10 gold coins. At such an occasion, the goldsmith had to have ten gold coins with him to return to depositors whenever they submitted the goldsmith's note. The balance ninety coins he could loan out. Taking this into consideration, the goldsmith could lend only ninety gold coins out of an incoming deposit of 100 coins, if he had to lend in gold at any given time.

2nd Example (scenario two)

People deposited 100 gold coins. In this scenario, the goldsmith did not issue gold to borrowers; he issued a note. People liked it because the note was honored by goldsmith when it was presented to him. At least that was what they believed.

Since he was not required to lend gold, he kept the total deposit of 100 gold coins as reserve. From his past experience, he knew that only 10 percent of note holders could possibly come to withdraw gold.

Since he had 100 coins—and if 10 percent of total notes he issued to depositors and borrowers (which is his total liability) are equal to 100—he could decide or calculate how many notes he could put into circulation.

Now assume he issued 100 notes to depositors and issued another 900 notes to borrowers. Now there are 1,000 notes in circulation. Out of this, possibly 10 percent of notes would return to the goldsmith by holders of the notes to withdraw gold. So, 10 percent of 1,000 is equal to 100. This means if 1,000 notes are in circulation, the goldsmith has to have actual gold coins amounting to 100. Since he did not lend any coins, the goldsmith has 100 gold coins in his reserve—and he can honor withdrawals without any problem.

In this second scenario, the goldsmith knows that his total liability should not exceed 1,000 if he operates at 10 percent cash (the word cash is important) reserve margin. In fact, he lent money he did not actually have. The total system depended on the trust people kept on the goldsmith.

Contrary to the second scenario, the goldsmith lent what he had in the first scenario.

Now, assume the rate of interest he charges is 8 percent. In the first scenario, he lent 90 gold coins out of an incoming deposit of 100 gold coins. So, he can earn seven gold coins (the exact figure is 7.2 coins) at the rate of 8 percent interest. In the second scenario, he lends 900 (in the form of notes) out of an incoming deposit of 100 gold coins. He earns seventy-two gold coins at the rate of 8 percent interest. His income has increased exponentially. If deposits are interest-bearing, then the goldsmith's profit can be a little lower than seventy-two.

Also there is a possibility that some notes would come back as deposits if the goldsmith paid interest for deposits. Assume that the goldsmith received a non-cash deposit (that means goldsmith's notes, not gold) of 100. From an incoming cash (gold) deposit of 100, he created credit up to 900. Now he has just received a non-cash deposit of 100. Can the goldsmith use this new incoming deposit to create credit for another 900 since he has 200 in deposits? No, the maximum amount of credit he could create in the form of notes relates to the cash reserve margin—and not to the total incoming deposits. However, in modern economies, the requirement of cash margin is diminishing because people use more and more checks, ATM debit cards, and credit cards to execute transactions. Theoretically at a cash reserve margin of zero, the possibility of creating credit by banks is infinite.

The system of banking in the first example can be defined as 100 Percent Reserve Banking or Full Reserve Banking. The rule is that the bank cannot lend more than what they have as incoming deposits.

The system of banking in the second example is called Fractional Reserve Banking. The rule is that the bank should only maintain a fraction of real cash reserve to the total liability. This is exactly how today's commercial banks operate. They really do not make money on your deposits. However, they need your cash deposit to create credit multiple times. That is how they create the money they lend.

The notes issued by a goldsmith to borrowers were indistinguishable from the notes he issued to depositors. Now, there are an additional 900 notes in the circulation, which means the money supply has increased. Those notes are money substitutes, and new money is created by the act of lending or creating credit. Hence, we call them "credit money."

Instead of goldsmith notes, today you replace it with bank endorsable checks. If the bank cannot issue checks or another money substitute, Fractional Reserve Banking is not possible. Instead of goldsmith's notes (a virtual money substitute), today we have checks backed by bank-maintained accounts.

However, it is easily misunderstood that each credit will become money. It is not. Each and every bank cannot do this type of money creation and participate in Fractional Reserve Banking. The first condition is that in order to create new money, the person who accepts the deposit should be able to create a money substitute. Only commercial banks can do it today. Their checks and money accounts act as money substitutes. Savings banks cannot create new money—even if they accept deposits and lend money—because they do not operate or are not supposed to operate checking (current) accounts. So, they cannot create a money substitute.

Technically, the banks that can participate in the Fractional Reserve Banking system are designated as commercial banks. So, savings banks and development banks do not fall into this category.

We saw above that the goldsmith has to do a balancing act daily. He must ensure that the notes he received should be honored. Let us assume that due to some reason more than 10 percent of note holders came to withdraw gold. But he has gold only to satisfy 10 percent of the notes. Then he has to borrow from another goldsmith who has deposits from his clients. The first goldsmith knows what is withdrawn would come back to him for safekeeping again. But until he gets back to his daily equilibrium, he has to borrow—and it is a temporary borrowing.

The same thing happens today among commercial banks. They call it interbank borrowing. This type of temporary borrowing is called "overnight" borrowing, and the rate of interest is a little higher and is called the "overnight rate."

If a lot of people came to withdraw gold, the goldsmiths can't honor them. They are bankrupt. This means the Fractional Reserve system is an inherently bankrupt system. This fact was clearly evidenced by the virtual failure of all big banks in the American system in 2008. Also you may remember one of the first actions taken to stabilize the American banking system was the declaration of FDIC (Federal Deposit Insurance Corporation). Usually FDIC guarantees the payment of deposits amounting to $100,000 or less. But in 2008 in order to prevent people withdrawing deposits fearing bank failures the FDIC declared that it undertakes to guarantee deposits up to $250,000 if any bank fails. Still it has been reported that "withdrawals exceed $1.5 trillion despite explicit government guarantees." (Edward Conrad, *Unintended Consequences, 2012*, p. 199).

The next important action was to open a lending window by the Federal Reserve to support the daily balancing act of banks—without which the failure of most banks were imminent.

Therefore, we have created Central Banks to safeguard the system. (Please note that Central Banks can safeguard the system only if macroeconomic fundamentals are in order. We will get to that later). So in order to ensure the smooth performance of the banking system in normal periods of economic activity, the Central Bank stipulates that a certain percentage of reserves should be held in the bank or must be kept with the Central Bank. This is what is known as Mandatory Reserve Ratio. In India, what should be held by commercial banks is defined as SLR (Statutory Liquidity Ratio), while the percentage of reserves that should be maintained with the Central Bank is known as Cash Reserve Ratio.

Apart from the MRR money, the banks have to have a cash reserve margin for the daily balancing act. If this margin is not sufficient for a short time period due to whatever reason, the bank can borrow from another bank at the "overnight" rate. If this is uncomfortable for any commercial bank, it could borrow from the Central Bank. A commercial bank has to go to the Central Bank to borrow because the bank fails to maintain a cash reserve margin for daily balancing act and also due to the fact that it cannot borrow from other banks, and it is a sign of weakness of the bank. Then in some countries Central Bank stipulates that the bank has to pay additional penalty for borrowing from the Central Bank if the number of borrowings exceeds a certain limit.

Perhaps now you may find how useful the story of goldsmith in order to understand the various aspects of Full Reserve and Fractional Reserve Banking systems. However please note the above historical story of goldsmiths is brought up here only to explain the concept behind the Fractional Reserve Banking system, but, in fact, it might have or might not have any value as a historical account.

You are now invited to compare the above explanation of Fractional Reserve system with the most authoritative report published on this subject. It is the MacMillan Committee Report of 1931. Below is the relevant quote from the MacMillan Report's version of Fractional Reserve Banking.

> It is not unnatural to think of the deposits of a bank as being created by the public through the deposit of cash

representing either savings or amounts, which are not for the time being required to meet expenditure. But the bulk of the deposits arise out of the actions of the banks themselves, for by granting loans, allowing money to be drawn on an overdraft or purchasing securities a bank creates a credit in its books, which is equivalent of a deposit. A simple illustration, in which it will be convenient to assume that all banking is concentrated in one bank, will make this clear. Let us suppose that a customer has paid into the bank £1,000 in cash and that is judged from experience that only the equivalent of 10 percent of the bank deposit need to be held actually in cash to meet the demand of customers; then the £1,000 cash received will probably support deposits amounting to £10,000. Suppose that the bank then grants a loan of £900 it will open a credit of £900 for its customer. And when the customer draws a cheque for £900 upon the credit so opened, that cheque will, on our hypothesis, be paid into the account of another of the bank's customers. The bank now holds both the original deposit of £1,000 and the £900 paid in by the second customer. Deposits have thus increased to £1,900 and the bank holds against its liabilities to pay out this sum (a) the original £1,000 of cash deposit and (b) the obligation of a customer to pay the loan of £900. The same results follow if the bank, instead of lending £900 to a customer, purchases an investment of that amount. The cheque which it draws upon itself in payment for investment is paid into the seller's bank account and creates a deposit of that amount in his name. The bank in this latter case holds against its total liability for £1,900 (a) the original deposit of £1,000 of cash and (b) the investment it has purchased. The bank can carry on the process of lending, or purchasing investments, until such times as the credit created or in investment purchased, representing nine times the amount of the original deposit of £1,000 in cash. (Page 34)

In the first sentence of the above quote, we have the word "deposits." If you make a deposit in a bank, you deposit part of your buying power; that is money. Then in the quote it is mentioned that "the £1,000 cash received will probably support deposits amounting to £10,000." This means now there is a cash deposit of £1,000 and £9,000 deposits created by the action of bank. Deposits are money, so we now have additional £9,000 as deposits, which mean new money created by bank's actions through lending or creating credit either to customers or to purchasing investments.

To create this new money nine times to the value of incoming deposit the bank has judged from past experience that only equivalent of 10 percent of the bank's deposit needed to be held actually in cash to meet the demand of customers who might come to withdraw in cash. Our goldsmith did the same thing. He held 10 percent in cash (gold coins) to create new money in the form of his notes amounting to nine times the incoming cash deposit.

With the above explanation of MacMillan Committee Report of 1931 and along with the Fractional Reserve System explained in above goldsmith story, we can conclude that even one bank could create more credit than the incoming deposit.

Please look at the very first chart in the book. You may now understand the mechanism of the creation of such an enormous banking assets; also you may understand the enormous amounts of liabilities that correspond to those assets. That is how private banking assets become a public problem in a crisis as observed by *Forbes*.

The goldsmith can't create new money if he has to lend in cash (gold coins) or if he has to keep cash to back up his total deposit liabilities, which is the rule of 100 Percent Reserve Banking. The creation of new money becomes possible only if a bank can operate at a fraction of reserves to its liabilities. If we want, we can covert the modern Fractional Reserve Banking practice to 100 Percent Reserve Banking system if designated commercial banks are requested by law to keep 100 percent reserves to back up total deposit liabilities. Under such a law, banks cannot create new money. So, checks and other electronic cards will be only instruments for convenience.

This is the reason I said that Section 4 of the Monetary Reform Act is correct theoretically.

Also as the banks cannot create credit to allow purchasing of so-called "financial investments" or financial assets, under a Full Reserve system, the speculation activity will be minimal.

But the theoretical accuracy of the methodology of conversion of the present system to Full Reserve system or minimizing speculative activity are not the consensual basis how we are going to determine which system we need to have in the economic system. The consensual basis to determine this question is whether the macroeconomic fundamentals demand a particular system.

In fact, macroeconomic fundamentals demand a very unique banking system. What is it? Let us look at this issue in the next chapter.

Chapter 3
System Gap Theory

A very simplified version of this theory has been presented in Chapter 1. As was mentioned in the introduction, simplified versions of economic theories are not sufficient to readers with analytical minds and for those who have academic objectives. This chapter to some extent will serve their needs since we define and prove the existence of System Gap in modern economic system.

This theory in macroeconomics is rather new. It was first published in 2008 in *Indispensable Bad Debt: The Theory of Economic System Gap and Credit Cycle*. Subsequently, an ex-World Bank economist who sent me reviews referred to this theory simply as SGT (System Gap Theory), which is the title of this chapter. Accordingly, the Theory of Economic System Gap and System Gap Theory refer to the same theory.

When somebody claims that he or she has conceptualized a new theory, it is required to explain the point of departure of the new theory from the existing ones. The point of departure of SGT from all other existing theories is quite clear from the hypothesis itself.

The starting hypothesis of SGT says, "The contemporary economic system can never pay consumers an aggregate income that is equal or exceeding to the value of consumption."

According to the above hypothesis, the economic system is not in natural equilibrium of demand and supply and, as such, consumers are required to consume beyond their aggregate income in order to have the economic equilibrium (demand-and-supply equilibrium). This has nothing to do with extreme consumerism because even with frugal consumption levels consumers are required to consume beyond their debt-free income. What is the effect of this kind of consumption? The effect is that the system should accumulate a component of non-repayable debt, which is simply bad debt. All economic and financial analysts now agree that major economic systems such as the US, Europe, and Japan have enormous non-collectable debt; in Japan, this situation became visible after its stock market crashed in the early 1990s. In the US and Europe, the current "bad debt" crisis surfaced after the Great Financial Crash of 2008.

In fact, the "crash" itself is the "effect" of a hidden cause if we look at the issue from the universal principle of "cause and effect." The hidden "cause" being the accumulation of non-repayable debt in the system resulted in creating credit to meet the demand-and-supply equilibrium. These bad debts accumulate in three specific areas in the economy: (1) household (private) consumption regime, (2) the government, and (3) stock and derivative market. Such accumulation of bad debt is camouflaged in the "complexity" of the economic system in those three areas but should surface during a crash. The crash is the resultant effect of the accumulation of unsustainable sum of bad debt.

Somebody might quickly think that consumption beyond income is bad—and if we can stop it, these bad debt crises would not arise. The problem is not that simple because consumption beyond income is a systemic requirement to ensure the economic equilibrium in the present. This equilibrium is necessary to ensure that entrepreneurs (producers) get back what they expect from consumers. If this does not happen, producers would reduce production leading to a recession as we noticed in the mechanics of recessions. (Please refer to Chapter 1.)

Not many economists identify a systemic contradiction. However, John Maynard Keynes observed the necessity in achieving the economic equilibrium (demand-and-supply equilibrium) to justify at any given amount of employment in order to induce entrepreneurs to offer the given amount of employment. In simple terms, this means that if employers make a loss, the economy is in crisis because employers reduce employment and output.

But Keynes did not point out that this equilibrium is met by consuming beyond income. Instead, he suggested that some kind of "conditional" investment or increasing the propensity to consume could bring this equilibrium.

Keynes said, "Employers would make a loss if the whole of increased employment were to be devoted to satisfying the increased demand for immediate consumption. Thus to justify any given amount of employment, there must be an amount of current investment sufficient to absorb the excess of total output over what the community chooses to consume when employment is at the given level. Unless there is this amount of investment, the receipts of the entrepreneurs will be less than is required to induce them to offer the given amount of employment." (*General Theory*, p. 27).

The above quote is important because one of the greatest myths that all economists believe is summarized in the passage. Let me explain this point after the proof of SGT as it is relevant for the subject that we discuss in this chapter.

Proof of the Existence of System Gap

(The following proof of the existence of economic System Gap was originally presented in *Indispensable Bad Debt* in November 2008).

In economics, we define the modern economy as "un-integrated economic system." In an un-integrated system, during any period of time, entrepreneurs will sell the finished output to consumers or to other entrepreneurs for a certain sum, which we will designate as A. Let us designate the amount sold to other entrepreneurs as A1.

Entrepreneurs will also have spent a certain sum, designated as A2, on purchasing output from other entrepreneurs. This includes all costs, such as raw materials, utility, and cost of machinery incurred by producing A except labor employed by the entrepreneur.

In addition, entrepreneurs spend a certain sum employing labor to produce A. Let us designate the cost of labor as L, which includes cost of labor of all kinds, including any remuneration paid to the entrepreneur for his consumption. Now, we can calculate the capital used on producing the output A.

Capital used up is equal to $A2 + L$.

Let us now define the consumption. Expenditure on consumption during any period must mean the value of goods sold to consumers during that period. In other words, it is the value of goods purchased by consumer purchasers, excluding purchases made by investor purchasers.

It is conceivable that it is not an easy task to differentiate consumer purchaser and investor purchaser.

"But this difficulty can be overcome when the consumption is defined as $(\sum A - \sum A1)$ where $\sum A$ is the total sales, and $\sum A1$ is total sales made by one entrepreneur to another. When we omit "$\sum$" we can write consumption as $(A - A1)$" (Keynes, General Theory, 1964, p. 62).

Anyway, this is just common sense. An entrepreneur sells his product either to consumers or to other entrepreneurs. Then, if we deduct from total sales the amount sold to other entrepreneurs, we will get what is sold to consumers. That is exactly what Keynes did above in defining consumption.

So, after defining the above two quantities, we can begin our analysis. Since the entrepreneur wishes to receive a higher income than the capital used up, we can write:

$A > (A2 + L)$

Where A is the total proceeds or income from the standpoint of entrepreneurs. $(A2 + L)$ is the total capital used up in a given period.

Then, $(A - A2) > L$

$(A - A2) - L > 0$ - - - - equation (1)

Both A and A1 are two unambiguous bookkeeping quantities. Consumer sales are not in books. That is why we define consumption through two calculable quantities. That is the logic behind the above definition of consumption. We need to define consumption and consumer income in calculable form in order to compare them.

In addition, in calculating the capital used up, we need to know what is bought from another entrepreneur. We defined that quantity as A2, and it is also an unambiguous bookkeeping quantity.

In fact, when we take one entrepreneur, both A1 and A2 are in his books, but, when summed up separately at the macro level, both are equal. Because A1 of entrepreneur X is posted in the books of buyer entrepreneur Y as A2. Similarly, A2 of entrepreneur X is posted in the books of Y or any other as A1. Therefore, $\sum A1 = \sum A2$. When we omit "$\sum$", we have A1 = A2.

From the above inequality equation (1), we know (A - A2)-L > 0.

Since A1 = A2, we can write (A - A1) - L > 0 - - - - (2)

We know from above, (A - A1) is the value of consumption and L is consumption money made available by all entrepreneurial activity or consumer income. Therefore, inequality equation (2) tells us that the value of what is available for consumption is greater than the money paid for consumers by all enterprises. There is a gap between consumer income and the value of consumption.

The said gap should exist in any economic system—no matter whether it is capitalist or socialist—if the economic system is money-based. Therefore, I define this gap as the economic System Gap. The gap arises from the need to expand capital immaterial of ownership of it or the entrepreneurs' requirement to receive a higher income than the capital invested. (A-A1)-L is the economic System Gap, and it is always greater than zero.

So, that we have now proved the hypothesis of SGT, which says, "The contemporary economic system can never pay consumers an aggregate income that is equal or exceeding to the value of consumption."

However, if the consumers did not purchase what is produced for consumption, then the production cannot continue, as the economic system is not in equilibrium. Therefore, the consumer liquidity must be equal to the value of consumption. In other words, consumers must spend a sum of money beyond their aggregate income so as to ensure that entrepreneurs get back what they expect from consumers. How do consumers do it having less income?

As we know, in the real world, some people save part of their income. At the same time, some people take credit for consumption. However, in order for the economic system to be in equilibrium, consumption must be equal to consumer liquidity or the amount they spent; as such, we can write:

(A - A1) = L - s + cr.

Where, s = consumer savings and cr = consumer credit.

Then, (A - A1) - L = cr. + s - - - - (3)

Above, we saw that (A - A1) - L is greater than zero (inequality equation 2). Therefore, the left side of the above inequality equation (3) must be greater than zero. Therefore, the right side of the above inequity must be greater than zero too.

Then, we have cr. + s > 0

cr. > s."

What does this mean? This means that the first equilibrium must always, in the long run, be met with a component of credit created exceeding consumer savings; as such, that component should accumulate and should become non-repayable at a certain point.

It appears that the above proof is appropriate for a producer economy, which does not have a large financial market.

As pointed out above, the System Gap is arising from the requirement to receive more income than what was invested. Does this requirement (or dynamic) change in a goods-producing economy with a large financial market? Of course it does not. Instead the contradiction between consumer income and the value of consumption should infiltrate into the financial market, needing to create more non-repayable debt in buying and selling of financial assets in deriving a relatively less consumable income. This bad debt in the financial market is temporarily hidden as sound investments, but during a collapse of the stock market, such bad debts would reflect from the credit defaults related to financial assets. The process of making debt in the stock market has been explained in Chapter 1.

Now let us get back to the point that we discussed before the proof of the existence of System Gap.

Though we found that the system should create more credit than savings in order for the entrepreneurs to receive what they expect from consumers, Keynes believed that continuing investments could ensure that employers would not make a loss. That means the economic system will be in equilibrium if investments are made subjected to one important condition according to Keynes.

That condition is that increased investments were not to be devoted to satisfying the increased demand for immediate consumption. If increased investments were to be devoted to satisfying the increased demand for immediate consumption then what happens? Keynes said, "Employers would make a loss if the whole of increased employment were to be devoted to satisfying the increased demand for immediate consumption." This means if investments are to produce commodities for immediate consumption, the economy is in crisis because employers would make a loss in such a situation.

That is why this question is so important. Let us investigate this matter.

Total output consists of two kinds of commodities. Some commodities are for immediate consumption. Other commodities are for the use of production, which are capital goods. In the final analysis, capital goods are in demand only to produce products for consumption whether for immediate consumption or in future consumption. This means all investments made in a real economy must be realized only from consumer sales whether it is immediate or in the future. If the investments are made to produce commodities for immediate consumption, the crisis is immediate—and if the investments are made to recover the investments in the future, the crisis will be in the future. That's the only difference. It is conceivable that differing mechanisms of crises would not work infinitely.

Let us understand this issue further with a numerical example.

In the economic system we noticed above, $A = A1 +$ consumer sales, whereas, A = total proceeds, $A1$ = sales for another entrepreneurs.

If, $A1 = 0$ then, A = consumer sales; this is an economic system where entrepreneurs do not sell to another entrepreneurs. This kind of system is known as a fully integrated economic system, but principles applicable to this system are equally applicable to our present system.

Therefore, in regard to a fully integrated system, let us assume that $500 is the capital used in the production and the value of the commodity output is $590. Original capital has now grown from $500 to $590. The $90 is the expanded capital.

Since the revenue is realized only from consumers in a fully integrated economic system, the value of consumer sales is $590 in our above example. The sum invested in production is $500, but since the producers do not buy from another producer, the amount invested in production must be spent to pay for the labor, and accordingly in the same period, $500 is the amount paid to labor, which means to consumers. This includes the entrepreneur's own consumption.

So, the system offered something for $590 to consumers. This is the value of consumption that the entrepreneurs expect to get back from consumers out of their expenditure. However, consumers were paid only $500. That means the system is not in equilibrium. There is a gap between what is available for consumption, which is higher, and consumer income. That gap is $90. This gap arises due to the requirement to provide for capital expansion, as we noticed above.

However, if this gap is not filled or if the system is not in equilibrium, capital expansion does not occur. Therefore, consumers must have $590 to do their consumption. How do they get the balance amount? They get it as consumer credit as explained by the System Gap Theory.

But Keynes believed that this equilibrium could take place with investments. If the expanded capital of $90 is invested in the current period and the produce is not available to be sold in the same period, then the system should be in equilibrium; $90 should go to labor that means to the consumer. In that case, we should account for the sales realized in the current period arising from the investments of the previous period too. Therefore, it is reasonable to ignore both, meaning the investment of expanded capital in the current period and the sales realized in the current period, arising by investing the expanded reserve capital in previous periods can be ignored reasonably. Accordingly, it is quite clear that even investments that do not produce products for immediate consumption could fill the System Gap; such investments widen the gap in the future. So we conclude that investments subjected to the Keynesian condition or without it do not play any role in filling the gap infinitely.

However, the above example clearly points out that the conditional investment proposed by Keynes is correct, but it is not a sustainable solution as it only helps to have a larger gap in the future.

So we can conclude that even "conditional investments" proposed by Keynes would not prevent employers from making a loss in the future. That means "conditional investments" are only a mechanism to postpone economic crises to the future.

The System Gap Theory clearly establishes that our economic system is not in natural equilibrium. Evidence shows that this disequilibrium is temporarily put into equilibrium by a component of bad debt created in the regime of consumption debt and in debt created in financial and asset markets. Unfortunately, there is no known mechanism to prevent systemic bad debt accumulation, which accumulation is proved by System Gap Theory and thereby leaving us with only one solution. That is the beauty of this contradiction because we have one solution: that solution being the periodic deflation of debt while keeping the "real aggregate consumer" income intact.

Let us discuss the solution to the systemic bad debt crises arising due to System Gap in detail in Chapter 8.

Chapter 4
The Two-Tier Production System

Professor Joseph Stiglitz is a former World Bank chief economist and Nobel laureate. He now teaches at Columbia University in New York. He wrote a book in 2010 which is titled *Free Fall* to explain the Great Recession of 2008, discuss the policy responses, and discuss solutions to prevent such crises.

In the book, he suggests something important to begin our discussion in this chapter. He said, "We will now have to reconstruct a society with a better balance between the role of government and the role of market. More balance can lead to a more efficient and a more stable economy." (*Free Fall*, p. 185).

A stable economy is not necessarily an efficient economy and vice versa. The stability of the economy relates to having the demand-and-supply equilibriums at the consumption level and total output level. But the efficiency of the economy more relates to the allocation of resources efficiently among various production processes.

The System Gap Theory proves that our economic system is not in natural equilibrium but requires to be put into equilibrium so as to ensure that employers would not make a loss at the macroeconomic level. This must be the primary role of the government.

The primary role of the market is to ensure the allocation of resources efficiently among various production processes.

Therefore what is now necessary is not to reconstruct a society with a better balance between the role of government and the role of market but to redefine the role of government and the role of market. You will be more enlightened about this subject in this chapter.

Achieving economic equilibrium by filling the System Gap is not all that we want. Filling the System Gap is crucially important for preventing economic recessions. But we also want to ensure the best possible efficiency in the economic system. In other words, we can have equilibrium in an inefficient economic system—or we can have equilibrium in efficient economic system. Our objective would be to have an economic equilibrium in an efficient system. In order to achieve this goal, we need to organize the production system in a particular way and, to do that, understanding the "two-tier production system" is essential. Hence this chapter will discuss about the structure of the production system.

In our macroeconomic system, a certain amount of money is allocated for the use of consumption—and a certain amount of money is allocated to be "money capital," which must be invested.

Money is money. There is no label attached to money as "consumption money" or as "money capital." It is exactly due to this very reason we can convert what is allocated to be "capital money" into "consumption money" or vice versa. In both cases, the economic efficiency suffers. Therefore, we need to understand the distinction between the two forms of money and how and when they are produced in the production cycle so that we will not interfere with the conversion of the forms of money arbitrarily.

We make a lot of mistakes in macroeconomic policy management in many areas due to lack of knowledge of the distinctive role of two forms of money.

For example, "consumption money" should be distributable in the economic system. Tax is a mechanism for redistribution. Therefore, "consumption money" should be taxed—not the "money capital." What the corporation holds is "capital reserve." Therefore, the macroeconomic impact is not the same when we tax "enterprises" or when we tax the household income of wealthy owners of the enterprises.

Let us take another example. Campaign financing of political parties is consumption money (you will find later why it is defined so). What a corporation holds after paying taxes and dividends is capital reserve. If a corporation donates to a political party, it becomes a conversion of "money capital" into "consumption money" because campaign finance is consumption money. If the corporation thinks that capital reserve is too much, such excesses must be converted into "consumption money" by paying the rightful owners of that money—the owners being the employees and equity holders of the company.

Therefore, corporations donating to campaign financing are a conversion of capital reserve into consumption money mode, which is wrong on a macroeconomic sense, while trade unions donating to campaign financing are a conversion of consumption money into consumption money, which is not wrong in macroeconomic sense (perhaps it could be morally wrong).

You may think that it is important to understand the distinction between two forms of money and how they originate. Finally, we will know how this knowledge can be used to increase the economic efficiency in our system. Let us investigate this subject now.

In a money-based economic system, some goods and services are produced for the market exchange and some are not. In other words, certain things are produced not to sell but for the use of common interest of people. The best example for the latter kind of "produce" is the law and order or judiciary service. In short, in the production system, we have one tier producing for market and the other tier producing things not to sell or buy. Therefore, these two tiers of production should exist in any money-based economic system. Concomitant arrangement of these two segments of production should be understood clearly.

In a money-based modern economy, production (or use of social resources for production) is basically done by two groups of people. One set of people produces products known as consumer goods and services or products for the use of production of those consumer goods. They use part of the available resources in the country. Let us refer to these producers as enterprises.

Enterprises offer their production to the market; hence, the consuming public validates their use of resources in the process of purchasing. If consumers do not purchase, entrepreneurs stop production of that particular item(s). That means the entrepreneur stops using physical resources, which are limited, on producing products that have no demand. Therefore, the market plays an important role—not only as a place of exchange but also as a point of validation for using social resources by enterprises. In addition, in that sense, the market is a highly efficient and democratic institution because the consuming public decides what the entrepreneur should produce.

The other group of people organized in an institution called the government uses another part of resources for production. Usually, as a rule, the products of the government, which are known as services, could not be sold for profit. For example, these services could be general administration of the country, law and order, research and development, or infrastructure development. In some countries, this list of services includes services such as education and health care. These services are produced by the government for the common interest and satisfaction of the society. By any chance, if the government produces a product or service that could be sold for profit or at a loss, the endeavor falls into the category of enterprises. However, that enterprise could be owned by the government.

Therefore, irrespective of ownership, we have enterprises on one side and the government on the other side as producers.

Now, the first group of producers (enterprises) uses money capital to employ the resources for production. They recover the capital invested, usually with a surplus, at the point of sale. Hence, the sale is a must for enterprises. Enterprises convert money capital into productive power during the production process in employing machinery, raw materials, utility services, and labor. Enterprises recover the capital invested through sales proceeds.

The other group of producers, namely the government (as per our above definition of the government) does not sell anything they produce. The government also uses money to produce services. Yet, this money is not recovered. Therefore, it should be different from the money capital used by enterprises. Primarily, capital has to be recovered through sales if it wants to be capital. Money expended by the government is not recovered and, hence, cannot be defined as capital even if part of the money is spent on so-called capital projects. Then what kind of money is spent by the government?

If you go to a restaurant and spend money to buy something to eat, do you call the money you spend capital? No, we do not call that money capital; it is used for consumption—and we name it "consumption money." When the money is spent on food, the money is gone—and you can't recover it. That is why household expenditures fall into the category of "consumption money." By this definition, what the government is spending is "consumption money" because the government cannot recover it through sales proceeds. Therefore, when the government spends on research and development, infrastructure, or on NASA, that expenditure cannot be economically defined as "investments for the future." They can be defined as "consuming for the future." This understanding is very important in macroeconomic administration.

You will further understand that we only define the money expended by the government as "consumption money" when the origin of governmental income and the true purpose of governmental expenditure are considered as we continue this discussion. However, it is worthy to mention here that because of the government's consumption, the economic system would produce services such as law and order, administration, research and development, and infrastructure development, which are essential for any society.

Now let us recognize the difference in the type of money both producers employ for production. Enterprises use money capital for production while the government uses consumption money for production. Basically, the money system has to provide money capital to enterprises and consumption money to the government to do the production. If the money system is capable of providing both these producers their "rational" share of money sufficient to employ the available resources almost fully and efficiently for production, the society should be satisfied with it because they have fully employed the available physical resources. However, rampant economic ills show that this is not happening around the globe. That is why we need to understand this two-tier production system thoroughly in order to identify the sources of funds and lapses of fund allocation to both producers because the "rational share of money" is not given but depends upon our policy decisions.

How does the economic system provide each producer their share of money? Previously, we mentioned that the services produced by the government are not sold and do not generate sales proceeds. Then, national revenue or proceeds should be generated only by enterprises. Then, at any given period of accounting, we have total proceeds generated only by enterprises—and not by any other entity.

The second group of producers, namely the government, does not generate any "real" proceeds. The government has a certain income, but it is not misunderstood as "proceeds," which generate only from a sale of a product or service.

Without sales proceeds, capital cannot exist. Let us examine what would happen to the capital used in the current production cycle. Capital is used to buy means of production like raw material, machinery, utilities, and labor. Also the enterprises pay taxes according to present arrangements since taxes are a cost of production and capital reserve is always a quantity after tax. Raw material cost is an income of another entrepreneur, and he pays labor and other costs of production. As it goes on, it is conceivable that the capital spent would be converted into two main things down the road—labor cost and tax—if any inefficiency did not tie up the capital flow.

Labor gets "consumption money." Let us make a small change in tax payments; the portion of tax payable by the enterprises is made to zero and that component of tax is added to the income (wages) of labor—and the labor is mandated to pay taxes. Accordingly, taxes are paid by labor of enterprises but not by the enterprise.

Out of the income of employees, they spend part of it on consumption. The other portion is to pay taxes. The tax portion goes to the government. The government pays its employees, welfare and pensions, which is converted into consumption money. Those employees produce services for the common interest. So, taxes get converted into consumption money through the government. So, it is clear that both wages of employees of enterprises and taxes are consumption money—and both are allocated from the entrepreneurial activity.

From the adjustment we made in paying taxes, we saw clearly that employees of enterprises pay taxes out of the consumption money and that tax money is converted into consumption money. Even if enterprises are made to pay taxes under the present arrangement, that is only a mere arrangement of changing the point of tax collection.

Let us investigate this matter further. Now, there are means of consumption to be distributed among producers in a given period. In other words, this is the distributable income available. However, we cannot pay or distribute everything to the direct producers who are the people involved in "enterprises." Out of this, we have to deduct for the government's consumption—first to provide for general administration, second for the products/services of the common interest, and third for welfare for those unable to work. We do these deductions by taxing the consumption money. After those deductions, the balance is to be distributed among the individual direct producers in the enterprises. This portion includes net wages (after tax) of direct producers, including consumption money paid to employers and owners. In short, what we do is deprive a certain amount of consumable income to direct producers (in enterprises) known as tax.

Therefore, clearly, tax is a part of income deprived to direct producers of enterprises. However, that money is expended in producing things of common interest by the government. Karl Marx explained this story of tax clearly. He said, "What the producer is deprived of in his capacity as a private individual, benefits him directly or indirectly in his capacity as a member of society." (www.marxists.org/archive/marx/works/1875/gotha/ch01.htm). This is the basis of taxation, and tax is a mechanism to distribute the means of consumption in any given period while producing common interests. I submit the quote of Marx because I could not find any better definition from capitalist economists to explain the real source of tax and the purpose of it.

Both wages to direct producers and taxes are consumption money. They originate in the cost incurred by enterprises (or proceeds generated and converted as capital by enterprises through market process). This is the first reason that we define the money expended by government as "consumption money." Even though taxes are to be originated by depriving certain consumable income to direct producers, for administrative purposes, the point of collection of taxes may vary.

For example, one might think that not only the employees of revenue generating enterprises are paying taxes, but also the employees of the government pay taxes. The simple explanation for this situation is that direct revenue-generating producers are paying taxes to enable the government to pay its employees a sum that includes a portion of disposable wage income and a sum for the payment of tax. Perhaps this arrangement might be useful to implement an equitable tax policy. But the ultimate truth is that only the revenue generators can pay real taxes in a two-tier production system.

Also we can impose a sales tax. Now our common perception is that the consumer pays sales tax. That is what we see happening. But, in macroeconomic sense, even sales taxes are paid by the producers. In order to understand this, let us assume that we do not impose sales tax; instead, the price of the product is set to be the price after the sales tax. In other words, sales tax is included in the selling price. So tax portion is an income of the enterprise, and the enterprise pays it to employees and owners; in turn, we let them pay the taxes. In such an arrangement, it is clear that revenue generators pay the taxes in reality, but for administrative purposes and other product sectorial necessities, we make adjustments to the point of tax collection. Whatever the case is, that tax is a deprivation of a part of consumable income to direct producers of enterprises.

Accordingly, as we saw earlier, that capital is produced by enterprises, and now we see consumption money also is made available to society by entrepreneurial activity, not by any other activity (except the amount of credit money required to fill the economic System Gap). Therefore, it is obvious that there must be an optimum enterprise base in the economic system to generate total proceeds. When the enterprise base is larger, total proceeds become larger and so are the capital and consumption money that flow from it.

When the enterprise base is bigger, the use of society's resources by enterprises is bigger. Therefore, the rest of the resources are small and available for government use, which requires less tax. When the enterprise base is smaller, then the taxation will be higher, and the market exchange of goods and services is small, thereby resulting in smaller total proceeds.

Since both capital and consumption money flow from total proceeds of enterprises, we have to optimize the generation of total proceeds that affect the efficiency of the system. Accordingly, when we decide the government budget, in fact, what we do is the change of the size of the each tier of the production system. Optimum size of each tier gives the best possible efficiency of the economic system. Accordingly, efficiency is a variable that depends on policy makers or macroeconomic decision makers. Because their decision is about a better balance between the size of government production and the size of market production then that can lead to a more efficient economy. The question of a stable economy is a different one that is not related to better balance.

We learned that enterprise activity creates an economic System Gap that must be filled to facilitate the generation of the intended total proceeds. Until this gap is filled, the intended total proceeds will not be realized. (Please refer to Chapter 6.)

However, the most important point is that no matter how efficient both tiers of production are, the system cannot eliminate the System Gap by its own. You can reduce taxes to increase the share of market order of production, but the System Gap still exists. You can increase the taxes, but the System Gap still exists because the enterprises that provide the total consumption money (direct wages cum taxes) cannot allocate the enough debt-free amounts for the consumers with a larger government or a smaller government.

Therefore, the discussion on the two-tier production system is about striking a proper balance between two tiers of production—only as a matter of having optimum economic efficiency—but definitely not as a matter of ensuring the stability.

That is why we reject the notion of Stiglitz when he says that more balance can lead to a more efficient and a more stable economy; a proper balance is good for efficiency at present but not for the long-term stability because stability is something to do with achieving equilibrium and achieving equilibrium has nothing to do with a proper balance between the government and market.

Therefore, do not make a mistake that achieving economic equilibrium is a question outside the purview of this two-tier production system and ensuring macroeconomic equilibrium must be the primary role of the government while ensuring economic efficiency by determining the optimum size of "out-of-market" production.

Chapter 5
Market Mechanism and Monetary Mechanism

The market process gives meaning to money and justifies its existence. In turn, the money system provides the infrastructural base for the market to function.

Money is not real but is an abstract quantity and can be produced as much as we wish. So it is accurate when Ben Bernanke intimated that the government can produce as many dollars at essentially no cost if it wishes to do so. However, it is conceivable that if the money system fails, the market mechanism should fail. That is why we should be careful with the money system.

When an economic crisis hits, most people believe it is a failure of the market order, but it is a failure of monetary mechanism. Therefore, understanding the role of the market mechanism and monetary mechanism is very important.

The word "market" is a complicated one. According to the basic definition, the market is a place where goods and services are offered for money and are purchased by money. This explanation is very clear, and there is nothing complicated about it.

Then what is a financial market? Financial markets are places where certain things are offered for money and bought with money. The things offered in financial markets are broadly known as capital and credit; a few examples might give you a clear idea about things exchanged in financial markets. Equity, bonds, derivatives, and currencies are some examples that are exchanged in financial markets.

The behavior, purpose, and operational aspects of the financial market and the goods and services market of the real economy are not the same. If I give you a quick example, the investments made in buying goods and services by an individual or a company are recorded in calculating the GDP (Gross Domestic Product) of a country, but investments made in financial markets are excluded (or not used) in calculating the GDP.

Therefore, when we talk about "market mechanism" it is necessary to specify which market we are talking about. When I use the words "market order," "market mechanism," or "market order of production," I am referring to the goods and services market of the real economy. In order to refer to the transactions of stock and derivative markets, we can simply use the term "financial markets."

It is better to start this discussion with a historical note. The US economy virtually crashed in 2008. In this crisis, speculators, unpatriotic entrepreneurs, and government corruption are sometimes cited as causes. For example, corporate heads of oil companies were summoned before two Congressional hearings in early 2008 in the United States. They were made to testify under oath. They were questioned about the net profit of their companies and personal earnings. Most of the questions were targeted to give the public an impression that the market mechanism (in the real economy) was failing. So, government intervention could be demanded to regulate market prices. Fingers were pointed at the wrong cause and demanded the wrong solution.

Yet, something was wrong with the economy because the economic system crashed. We need a solution. The first thing we have to do is to find the real cause. That is the key to finding a viable solution. So, which is at fault? Is it the market mechanism or the monetary mechanism? This is what we are going to investigate in this chapter.

Micromanagement of the economy by the government is not possible. No government is big enough to micromanage the economy. Regulations cannot be the way to manage economy. That is the truth. Instead, we need a system to be put in place. In such a system, single government policy decisions would direct resources, including capital, to wherever they needed to be allocated. This must be the basis. Any regulatory and administrative measures should only be complementary to that system.

What is the best system? Make no mistake; it is the market order. We know the market economy is blamed when there is an economic recession, price instability, inflation, and unemployment. This is entirely wrong. We do not identify the real cause for disturbances in the economy; instead, we attack the market mechanism, which is the best planning tool ever evolved by human kind.

This is not just capitalist ideology. Leon Trotsky said, "Market and credit mechanism serve the cause of socialism better than capitalism." Therefore, we need to investigate how the "market order" of production needed to be treated as a planning tool of allocating resources among various kinds of production processes. Let us look at this issue from fundamentals.

Both socialists and capitalists can agree on one important goal: we need to have an economic system to produce goods and services efficiently and to distribute the consumable output efficiently among members of the society. The key word is efficiency. Marxist philosophers submitted that the capitalist system is inefficient in achieving the said objectives—but socialism is a more efficient system. Capitalists argue otherwise. Some so-called pragmatists argue the best ideas of both systems would make a better system and that system they call a "mixed economic" system. In fact, what is the most efficient system?

Let us start with capitalism. There are certain amounts of productive resources in any given country. Those resources are used in the production, and such resources are limited. Hence, resources should efficiently be allocated among numerous product areas. Capitalist philosophers argue that resource allocation is highly efficient under "market order" of production—when the economy is set up on demand-and-supply basis. This is the first point.

Then they argue that human creativity is vital in the project of pursuing economic growth, and human creativity (including entrepreneurship) would be better under the private ownership of the means of production (such as factories) including money capital. Private ownership is the second point.

They further argue that the market mechanism would be more efficient if the value of every product can be expressed in one single unit of measure called money. In order to cater for this requirement of money, capitalists established a highly organized, flexible money system, currently under Fractional Reserve Banking System. This is the third element of capitalism.

The above three basic elements constitute the capitalist system.

So what are the key elements in a populist socialist economy? Let me present them with a comparison to a capitalist system.

(1) Central Planning of Production (not market order of production)
(2) Workers' ownership of means of production (not private ownership)
(3) Elimination of money or near elimination of the role of money through price controls (not real flexible money)

Until the Soviet Revolution took place in 1917, the concept of "socialism" was a utopian one. After the Soviet Revolution, the question of establishing an efficient economic system became a practical one; they abolished private ownership of means of production and put central planning in place, yet in the early years of the revolution, money was not fully abolished. Within a few years of revolution, Soviet Russia saw its first excessive inflation. Trotsky named it "socialist inflation." The Soviet regime responded by literally abolishing the use of money and by introducing excessive price controls. Labor was paid by various merchandise cards. This happened in early 1930s. Soon workers did not want to work as their payment was not related to their labor output and not paid based on their work. The Soviet regime used the military to ensure that workers worked and, as a result, workers' rights were suppressed. The whole system became a flop, and the use of money in paying for labor was reintroduced in mid-1930s—but with excessive price controls. Since then, until the Soviet system collapsed in 1991, it remained as very inefficient economic system—even though it became a military superpower after World War II.

Leon Trotsky foresaw this mistake. This should be the very reason that Trotsky did not identify the market order of production as wrong. Trotsky said, "Market and credit mechanism serve the cause of socialism better than capitalism." He criticized price regulations. Attacking the Soviet regime's excessive price controls, Trotsky explained the reasons for his views.

He said, "The professors forgot to explain how you can estimate real costs if all prices express the will of a bureaucracy and not the amount of socially necessary labor expended. And as to prices, they will serve the cause of socialism better, the more honestly they express the real economic relations of the present day" (Leon Trotsky, *The Revolution Betrayed*). In this quote, "the professors" mean the economic professors of the Stalin regime.

Perhaps, some socialists might reject Trotsky's views, saying that those are not Marxist views, but then they must turn to Karl Marx to see what his views were on this point.

Marx said, "The actual sale of commodities for money tests the validity of the expectation that any particular labor expended is indeed social and necessary labor. It is only after sale that the social and necessary character of the labor expended in producing a commodity is guaranteed. The commodity producer produces the commodity on a speculation that the market will validate the social and necessary character of that labor." (*Marx's Theory of Money in Historical Perspective*, Duncan K. Foley, November 1, 2003) (https://www.mtholyoke.edu/courses/fmoseley/conference/foley1.pdf)

So, Marx—as well as Trotsky—points out the requirement of validation of expended labor in order to ensure whether that amount of labor is used usefully; the mechanism for such validation is the market exchange of produce. This validation is required not only to the labor expended on production but also to all other productive resources.

Such validation is only possible after the sale of a commodity. That is the role of market mechanism.

Therefore, when we have a system to express the value of almost all goods in one single unit of measure (i.e. money) and when we accept the market order of production as the main system, by these two measures, we quickly resolve the major problem of macroeconomic planning of production because the market mechanism flexibly determines the quantity, quality, and variety of almost all products and services under demand-and-supply basis. Even the most sophisticated central planners can never do this more efficiently than market mechanism. For example, can the central planners determine how many iPods or iPads will be produced and determine who should consume them? Forget about iPads—just think whether the Central Planners can determine how much "Chinese fried rice" from different varieties and quality can be produced by restaurants.

This is not capitalist thinking. I now find that there are thinkers in capitalist camps whose enthusiasm in market mechanism is fading after the great crash of 2008. This is because they could not differentiate the market order of production from the "financial market." In fact, market mechanism is a planning tool. This is a fundamental fact in economics. Therefore, the ideological difference between true socialists and capitalists cannot be based on the market order of the economy. As such, the debate should not be about the enthronement or dethronement of the market mechanism. However, this debate existed and continues to exist. It is a false and useless debate.

The consumer has to validate the production by the act of purchasing. By doing that, consumers decide which branches of industry or services should use the scarce resources in the country. It is not certain whether devoted capitalist economists could find a better theoretical reason to explain the role of the market than above. Marx's words on this point are enlightening.

The allocation of society's physical resources among various production processes are needed to be done efficiently. The market mechanism is an essential tool to do this. In other words, the market mechanism is the best planning tool when we refer to macroeconomic system.

Leon Trotsky recommended this principle be applied in the young Soviet Union under a different framework of capital ownership. His attack on price regulations was not a mistake. He further wrote, "Directive prices were less impressive in real life than in the books of scholars." (*Revolution Betrayed*). If entrepreneurs (or producers) had good luck in the price mechanism of the market, then Trotsky had a solution. He said, "In reality, for the redistribution of the people's income the government has in its hands such mighty levers as taxes . . . the budget and credit mechanism is wholly adequate for a planned distribution of the national income" (Leon Trotsky, *The Revolution Betrayed*). The important point is he did not advocate "administrative" prices in general.

Ironically, Stalin—the ruler in the Soviet Union after Lenin—decided otherwise. In the early 1930s, Soviet Russia issued various cards, such as bread cards and industrial merchandise cards. That was the first experiment made by a relatively advanced industrialized country to eliminate the market mechanism and money. In just about two years, the whole system failed—the role of money was accepted and the market exchange of goods revived but not to the full extent of a free market but with directive prices that set the cause for economic inefficiency.

In view of the above discussion, we converge into one thing: there cannot be a debate in using the market mechanism to produce consumer goods and services. That is the only efficient way to do it.

Immaterial of the ownership of ventures, prices should reflect the market reality. Then, what should we really be debating? It is nothing other than how the market mechanism is best used to create optimum or maximum wealth and be distributed the distributable output according to the cultural norms of any particular society.

However, as we all know, the so-called market economies do not deliver what they promise. They are infected with inflations, recessions, occasional depressions, and unemployment. The true cause for these illnesses is not in the market mechanism but in the money system, without which the market order cannot prevail.

As I mentioned at the beginning, the market process gives the meaning to money and justifies its existence. In turn, the money system provides the infrastructural base for the market to function. The money system should ensure that economic equilibriums at consumption level and total output level are met in order to ensure that enterprises (entrepreneurs) would not make a loss at macroeconomic level. Please note that at a micro level, a particular enterprise would make a loss under market order. This is required in order to redirect productive resources to another useful production process. Even this happens under the demand-and-supply basis—based on consumer preference at the microeconomic level, the equilibrium at the macroeconomic level would be intact. (Please refer to Chapter 1.)

However, from the System Gap Theory, we know that the macroeconomic equilibrium breaks if the System Gap is not filled. Therefore, it requires the filling of System Gap in a sustainable manner, putting the economic system into equilibrium in order to continue production under the market order. The System Gap itself originates from the market order of production but needed to be filled by a mechanism outside the market process; this bridging mechanism is in the money system. When the money system cannot do this job properly, it surfaces as a problem in the market mechanism.

That is why the market order of production in general is not at fault. The market order by itself cannot go into a disorder. Only monetary disorder can put the market order into disorder. This was what happened in the Great Recession of 2008. So, we understand that the monetary system in which financial markets play a significant role was at fault for the Great Recession of 2008.

Perhaps, those who demand strong regulations for financial markets might pick the above conclusion to justify their demands. However, I do not intend to discuss the subject of financial market in this chapter. I wish to clarify one point in regard to regulating financial markets.

If free market mechanism should prevail in the real economy, why do the same principles not apply to the financial markets? I do not think that we should regulate the financial markets. Instead, they should be deregulated. As of now, there is a rule or regulation that allows commercial banks (the banks that can create credit money by participating in the Fractional Reserve System) to credit finance the stock and derivative purchases. The best deregulation is to remove this rule. If we stop the credit financing of stocks by commercial banks (which means that commercial banks do not sponsor for stock purchases direct or indirect), we can let the stock and derivative markets function as freely as possible. Now the stock and derivative markets are free. We might need only a few regulations to stop personal malpractices.

This simple "deregulation" will ensure the free market principles in financial markets and also will eliminate the speculative bubbles to necessary levels. In other words, it will stop the disorderly behavior of financial markets. After this deregulation, the stock market would revert to performing the true economic purpose, which is to provide a temporary place to invest capital reserves or savings. Thereafter, the stock purchases have to be done only on savings of the system. In fact, the real regulation is to allow the commercial banks to create credit under Fractional Reserve System for stock purchases—and this practice should be abolished in order to allow financial markets to be free. But this deregulation must be effected if we wish to do so—as a global convention to put all countries on an even playing field.

Turning back to our main topic, we know that the System Gap exists under normal circumstances in any market economy at any level of development. Here "normal circumstances" mean that the country carries no excessive trade surpluses in the long run.

However, this gap has to be bridged to put the economic system into equilibrium in order to continue production in accordance with the given physical capacity of production being free from crises.

Therefore, the true debate must be on which system and under which institutional and political framework could a healthy System Gap be created and bridged efficiently, flexibly, and in a sustainable manner to create optimum wealth for any given nation and to distribute the distributable wealth (income) as it suits for the country's cultural norms.

This is the true debate that all kinds of politicians, economists, and the population at large should be engaged in. This type of debate is not ideologically based. It has a true scientific basis. Because of the scientific nature of this debate, at the end of it, dogmas in regard to economic management would vanish—and a scientific model for macroeconomic policy management would emerge.

Chapter 6
Achieving Economic Equilibriums or Filling the System Gap

According to the mechanics of recessions, the macroeconomic system should be in demand-and-supply equilibrium to be recession free. (Please refer to Chapter 1.) In other words, entrepreneurs or employers would not make a loss when the system is in equilibrium so that they would not reduce employment and output.

But our practical problem arises from the fact that the economic system is not in a natural equilibrium. Some mainstream schools of economic thought believe that the economic system can achieve its equilibriums through market forces and System Gap Theory (SGT) disproves this notion beyond any doubt.

Before the conceptualization of SGT, John Maynard Keynes observed that the macroeconomic system is not in natural equilibrium; in other words, employers would make a loss if the investments or the propensity to consume is not increased. However, his suggested investment in order to achieve equilibrium is subjected to one important condition. That condition is that the investment must not produce commodities for immediate consumption. This means any kind of investment would not put the system into equilibrium. Accordingly, it is clear that he observed that the economic system is not in natural equilibrium; the system must be put into equilibrium by increasing the propensity to consume or by increasing a particular kind of investment as pointed out above—or by both actions.

It is interesting and important to analyze Keynes's views because it is the only mainstream school of economic thought that demands government intervention when the system breaks its equilibrium. However, Keynesianism identifies the wrong kind of cause for the systemic disequilibrium and proposes the wrong kind of intervention.

Economists who hide behind business cycle theory to explain macroeconomic cycles should find that the development of physical productive forces is not cyclical, but we have a macroeconomic system that follows boom-and-bust cycles. If the development of physical productive power behaves in a boom-and-bust cyclical pattern, we have to tolerate the boom-and-bust cycles of macroeconomic output. But if the progress of the physical productive power or even if the potential of the increment of physical productive power is progressive, it is not necessary for us to tolerate the cyclical behavior of the macroeconomic system. This does not mean to say that the business cycles of microeconomic systems (which correspond to the performance of individual enterprises) should not be tolerated; instead, such cyclical behavior is necessary to ensure business efficiency, which is based on consumer preferences. Businesses should be allowed to fail—and new businesses should be allowed to emerge—based on efficiency and consumer preferences. But macroeconomic systems fail not due to consumer preferences but due to the general illiquidity of consumers arising from a bad debt crisis as explained by the System Gap Theory. The illiquidity of consumers is not a physical phenomenon but a monetary phenomenon; money that is not real is an abstract quantity that we can change prudently to serve the economy. Therefore, the macroeconomic cycle can be ironed out if consumers' periodic illiquidity problems are resolved, which is possible. I think SGT has provided a good answer to those economists who presume in their analyses that the system is in equilibrium subjected to business cycle behavior. Therefore, views of those schools are in error and are not necessary to discuss here.

Keynes did not believe that the economic system is in natural equilibrium. That is why analysis of his views is important.

Let me summarize Keynes's hypothesis in simple terms.

There is an employee who earns wages to satisfy his basic family needs. As the income is just sufficient to meet the cost of essentials, he spends almost all his money for consumption. Now as the economy grows, his income increases. But out of the increased amount, he does not require to spend all the money so he begins to save. Apply this psychological law of saving to aggregate income now. As the result of consumer saving, the entrepreneurs will not get back what they expect from consumers because the psychology of consumers is such that when the real income is increased, they do not increase the consumption by the same amount. The savings are done by consumers, but the demand is less than the output; in other words, the system is not in equilibrium. Employers will cut jobs and reduce output if two things do not take place. One is that the propensity to consume has to be increased. This means if consumers increase consumption by the same amount as the increased amount of income, employers would not make a loss—and the system is in equilibrium.

Or else, since there are savings, the saved amounts have to be used to increase investments that do not produce commodities for immediate consumption. Investments will employ new labor—and those people will increase consumption of what is already produced. Due to this conditional investment, the value of immediate consumption is not increased, but that will increase the consumption of what has already been produced—employers will not make a loss or the system is in equilibrium.

In order not to make any discrimination toward Keynes, let me quote him.

> The outline of our theory can be expressed as follows. When employment increases, aggregate real income is increased. The psychology of community is such that when aggregate real income is increased, aggregate consumption is increased—but not by so much as of income. Hence employers would make a loss if the whole of increased employment were to be devoted to satisfying the increased demand for immediate

consumption. Thus, to justify any given amount of employment, there must be an amount of current investment to absorb the excess of total output over what the community chooses to consume when employment is at the given level. For unless there is this amount of investment, the receipts of the entrepreneurs will be less than is required to induce them to offer the given amount of employment. It follows, therefore, that given what we shall call the community's propensity to consume, the equilibrium level of employment, i.e. the level at which there is no inducement to employers as a whole either to expand or contract employment will depend on the amount of current investment. (Keynes, *General Theory*, page 27.)

Now let us compare Keynesian theory with SGT. Keynesian view is that a certain gap between demand-and-supply of total output arises due to increased savings by consumers because, as the aggregate income of consumers increases, they do not increase the consumption as much as income. If this is true, when the systemic economic crashes take place due to the breaking of demand-and-supply equilibrium, there should be a glut of savings when the equilibrium breaks. But evidence suggests otherwise: the equilibrium breaks due to the failure of credit mechanism due to heavy debt incurred by private consumers, or incurred by stock and derivative markets with an intention to derive certain income for the use of consumption or due to sovereign debt failure by the government again government expenditure goes for consumption. So, failure of credit mechanism is linked to bad debt, which is linked to consumption. So, systemic economic crashes are linked to bad debt—not to a glut of savings.

Contrary to the Keynesian view, SGT proves (not assumes) that the economic system can never pay consumers an aggregate income that is exceeding or equal to the value of consumption. The demand-and-supply equilibrium at the consumption level is temporarily met by a portion of bad debt created in the above three areas, which should accumulate during the period of growth and systemic crashes occur due to bad debt. Apart from the proof of theory, this notion is supported by the evidences of the great crash of 2008 and subsequent events in the US and Europe. Accordingly Keynes's psychological law derived by the observation of the behavior one single household is not applicable on the macroeconomic level.

However, the above conclusion is not what we are interested in discussing in this chapter. Instead, we are interested in investigating whether Keynes's conditional investment can put the system into equilibrium to ensure that employers would not make a loss.

It is conceivable that all investments made in the "real" economy have to be recovered, in the final analysis, through consumer sales. Keynes observes if the current investments produce commodities for immediate consumption, employers would make a loss because the receipts would be less than the output. But he further observes that if the current investments do not produce commodities for immediate consumption, employers would not make a loss. In other words, the economic system is in equilibrium. However, the produce of current investments has to come in the future for the use of consumption. Even with Keynes's conditional investment proposal, we can only postpone the breaking of economic equilibrium but not resolve the breaking of it. (Please refer to Chapter 3)

However, the macroeconomic system is not always in crisis. In certain periods, the economy grows. This means that we achieve economic equilibrium or filling of the economic System Gap at increasing output levels. Therefore, there must be some mechanisms in filling the System Gap in periods of growth. In fact, there are certain mechanisms that fill the System Gap to facilitate economic growth. But none of these mechanisms can fill the System Gap infinitely—and that is the reason for systemic economic crises.

Let us now look at the temporary mechanisms that fill the economic System Gap in periods of growth. There are three main mechanisms: (1) Investment of self-expanded capital and producer credit (2) Making money from money (stock and derivative market) and (3) Consumer credit (including private consumer credit and the government's deficit financing).

1) Investment of self-expanded capital and producer credit

When the expanded capital or capital reserve and the capital advanced by banks as producer credits are invested, new groups of people (new employees) become consumers or the income of existing workers might go up. That would increase the aggregate consumer income that contributes to fill the System Gap at present. But these investments are subjected to one important condition. The investment should not produce commodities for immediate consumption. (Refer to Chapter 3 for more details.)

However, all investments made in the so-called "real" economy have to be recovered, in the final analysis, through consumer sales. Therefore, when the production of new investments comes in the future, it would create a greater gap.

As pointed out in the preceding discussion, even though investment of savings as typified by self-expanded capital or producer credits could fill the gap today, it will create a greater gap tomorrow.

Accordingly continuing investments cannot put the economic system into equilibrium in the long term—even though this process is beneficial—as long as physical productive potential is utilized. So, the conclusion is that investments that do not produce commodities for immediate consumption fill the System Gap temporarily.

2) Making money from money in the stock market.

We create new money in the stock market. It is naive to believe that all investments made in buying stocks are from savings coming from the "real" economy. Through the Fractional Reserve System, we create new money without any relation to the "real" economy when commercial banks lend money to buy stocks. Usually a good percentage of the value of the current holding of stocks could be granted as an investment credit. These investment credits create new demand for stocks and push the prices of stocks up. These investments are realized through buying stocks at a lower price and selling them at a higher price; investors receive new income and part is used for consumption. Thus the money created outside the production process of the real economy and having invested in the stock market contributes to fill the System Gap.

Former Federal Reserve Chairman Allan Greenspan once said that one dollar out of each four dollars invested in the stock market goes for consumption.

But this mechanism of deriving consumer income is not sustainable because, to take some profit out, stock prices have to go up and derivatives have to expand. That means it has to create a bubble in the stock market and requires an expansion of stock market through derivatives. Concomitantly, there should be a debt bubble too because investments in the stock market are not purely coming from savings—rather it is a heavily debt-based process. (Please refer to Chapter 1.) The system allows commercial banks to extend credit to purchase "investments" (stocks). Hence, such upward price bubbles and expansion of derivatives cannot be sustained indefinitely. These upward price bubbles can spill into the property sector too. But properties are part of real economy. Bubbles could contribute to the upward movement of the prices of houses, commercial properties, etc. These prices should eventually reflect production and consumption, making the consumer credit mechanism unsustainable rather quickly.

Therefore, stock and asset bubbles could fill the System Gap today, but it makes a greater crisis of filling the System Gap when crashes occur. This is the most unsustainable mechanism in filling the System Gap.

Also due to high leverage of bank credit in the stock and derivative market, a reduction of stock prices could trigger defaults. Such defaults could threaten the stability of the banking system because the system is based on Fractional Reserve System.

Therefore, we conclude that ensuring the filling of System Gap through upward price bubbles in stock and derivative markets is only a another temporary mechanism.

3) Creation of consumer credit beyond their collective savings.

Consumer credit mechanism is the most important mechanism in filling the System Gap. Consumer credit consists of two components: private consumer credit and deficit spending of the government.

In the economic system, there is certain consumable income allocated to consumers. Private consumers and the government as an institutional consumer use that money. System Gap Theory proves the value of consumables is higher than consumable income. Therefore, consumers have to live beyond their monetary means to ensure that employers would not make a loss to ensure that the economic system is in equilibrium. The private consumers live beyond their debt-free income when they borrow more than what other consumers have saved collectively. The government lives beyond its income through deficit financing. Both such borrowings are made possible because of the Fractional Reserve Banking system.

But we already know that if a household consumes beyond its income, that family should accumulate bad debt and should bust after a certain period. The same is applicable to the aggregate debt of private consumers and the deficit spending of the government.

Therefore, we can conclude that the consumer credit mechanism temporarily fills the System Gap; the consumer credit mechanism is capable of putting the economic system into equilibrium temporarily.

Unfortunately, any one of the above three mechanisms or combination of them could not fill the System Gap in the longer term. In fact, we do not have any known mechanism to sustain the bridging of System Gap in the longer term. That is why we need to look outside the normal production system in order to find a solution. We discuss that solution in Chapter 8.

Before I finish this chapter, I wish to submit a quote attributed to a president of the United States who earned a reputation for mismanaging the Great Recession of 1929-1933. His name is President Herbert Hoover; by professional training, he was an engineer.

He said, "Even bad debt is good credit." Even though the common-sense understanding of his comment is negative, we see that it is a great observation that has been proven by the SGT. His observation is great subjected to one important condition: if the deflation of debt is done in the system in general—in the right time.

The truth does not need to be complicated. In fact, the truth is simple.

JAPAN GOVERNMENT DEBT TO GDP
Percentage of the GDP

Year	% of GDP
2000	135.4
2001	143.7
2002	152.3
2003	158
2004	165.5
2005	175.3
2006	172.1
2007	167
2008	174.1
2009	194.1
2010	200
2011	211.7

SOURCE: WWW.TRADINGECONOMICS.COM | MINISTRY OF FINANCE JAPAN

Part 2
Analysis of Some Policy Issues and the Solution

Chapter 7
Resolving Some Economic Policy Issues

Policy Question 1
Tax Cuts for Job Creators!

"Corporations are people, my friend." This was said at a meeting in August 2011 by Mitt Romney, the likely presidential candidate of Republican Party of the United States for the presidential election in 2012. Some people who were sitting in the front of the audience shouted, "No, they're not!" This argument took place when Mitt Romney tried to defend tax cuts to corporations.

The argument intimates that agitators wanted to increase taxes on corporations—and Romney did not.

The heated exchange prompted an attack from Democratic National Committee Chairwoman Debbie Wasserman Schultz. "Mitt Romney's comment today that 'corporations are people' is one more indication that Romney and the Republicans on the campaign trail and in Washington have misplaced priorities," she said in a statement, calling the comment a "shocking admission." Accordingly, the views of the people who shouted that corporations were not people were supported by one of the largest political parties in the US.

About nine months later, the incumbent President Obama was ridiculed for his comments. So, it seems that this is a policy matter unresolved. This is not only a debate in the US; this issue is debated around the world.

Let us investigate the appropriateness of this argument and counterargument using the theoretical understanding that gained in Part 1 of this book.

In general, Republicans are of the opinion that tax cuts granted to wealthy Americans and corporations would create jobs. That may be the reason they articulate their position as "tax cuts to job creators."

What is the first condition that is necessary to create jobs? According to the mechanics of recessions, if entrepreneurs (or enterprises) do not get back what they expect from the expenditure of consumers, they cannot increase employment. Instead, they reduce employment. Therefore, the first condition to create jobs is that employers should not make a loss.

Now, who are the employers? A majority of employers have a distinct legal identity called "enterprises." These enterprises could be large, small, or medium corporations—or even sole proprietorships.

Individuals who own these enterprises are not employers in a macroeconomic sense. Therefore, taxing enterprises and taxing owners of the enterprises will not have the same effect in the economy or job creation. During the discussion in this chapter, you will understand that it is wrong to tax "employers" (enterprises or corporations) and why it is wrong not to tax wealthy owners of enterprises.

The surplus the enterprises hold is capital reserve if the capital reserve is converted into productive power in the present or in the future. (Please refer to Chapter 4.) The capital reserve is there to invest to expand businesses and in the process to provide more employment and if labor market is saturated to increase productivity and wages or do both processes at the same time. That's the money that goes to create jobs. Such money is called capital reserves or expanded capital. If this money is not used currently by the enterprises then such money is made available to another person by banking system, who takes the risk to use it and pay an interest price.

Let us take a hypothetical example to get this point clarified further. Now, assume Berkshire Hathaway Incorporation (a large corporation) make a profit before tax. Since we do not tax "employers" the company Berkshire Hathaway does not have to pay taxes. So, it's after tax profit equals to the profit before tax. Out of this profit the company declares dividends to owners and part of the profit is kept as capital reserve.

What is paid for the owners from the profit is not capital money; instead the money owners get is "consumption money." With this money they should consume in order to facilitate to achieve economic equilibrium or should save if they have excesses so that another consumer can borrow it or perhaps they can buy equity in the market. Even purchase of equity from market by using household income is not an investment according to macroeconomic fundamentals because such investments are mere change the hands of equity holding. So, what any household can do from its income is to consume or to save. The only exception is that if the household start a new business or expanding an existing one by using part of their income then only that part becomes an investment which goes to create jobs and increase national revenue. I do not think any wealthy household is doing the later. So, in practical sense the most of the household income of wealthy Americans are not invested and hence cannot create jobs.

You may remember that as we explained in two-tier production system (Chapter 4), tax is consumption money and tax should come from household income. Therefore, for an example we tax the household income of Warren Buffet (who, in fact, expressed his willingness to be taxed as any other middle class Americans) who is one of the owners of the Berkshire Hathaway Corporation we tax the consumption money and not the capital. Because, what the company kept is capital reserve and what Warren Buffet got was consumption money. Now, assume that his household income was taxed like any other middle class American. Will such taxation affect the performance of Berkshire Hathaway Corporation? Not at all, but perhaps the company might do better as an employer because such taxation might contribute to stabilize the macroeconomic environment.

A friend of mine who works in Wall Street said that he did not understand this argument of capital money and consumption money. He said money is money and expenditure is expenditure whoever makes it. Let me put his argument in his own words. He said "if a company buys a lawn-mover the company spends money. Also if I buy a lawn-mover for my house I spend money. In both instances a lawn-mover was purchased from money and from the same store. So, how do we differentiate what is capital money and what is not?" This is a truly honest question. The answer is simple; the cost incurred by the company has to be recovered and the money spent by him would not be recovered, so that the money spent by company becomes capital and the money spent by my friend becomes "consumption money." Consumption money is the money or wealth that can be distributed. Capital money is there not for the distribution but for the investment and in the process to create jobs. (Please refer to Chapter 4.)

Whether you purchase the lawnmower or your neighbor purchases it does not matter for the efficiency of economy. It matters for the economic efficiency if the choice for the purchase is between the enterprise and your household. If the company purchases the lawnmower, the proceeds of the country would increase from which capital money and consumption money flow into the economic system. This won't happen if the lawnmower was purchased by your household instead of the company.

Therefore, according to the macroeconomic fundamentals, the wealth of "enterprises" is not for distribution; it is household income that becomes distributable wealth (income) and through taxation policies most appropriate distribution of distributable income (that corresponds to distributable output) could be effected without any negative impact for the economic efficiency of the system. Such redistribution promotes economic efficiency and social harmony. But if we tax the capital reserve, that will be bad for the economy. This is the macroeconomic arrangement we need to have in our economy to ensure efficient job creation.

Accordingly, we must support cutting taxes for job creators (enterprises) but not the household income of wealthy individuals who own enterprises.

During the presidential election of 2012, the likely nominee of the Republican Party is going to be Mitt Romney when I am writing this book. He is to contest Barack Obama of the Democratic Party. As said above, Mitt Romney had once said "Corporations are people." He was ridiculed strongly by President Obama for his statement.

You may define corporations as people or not, but definitely corporations are not consumers—and that's the very reason that they should be exempted of paying taxes.

From the above discussion, you might think that both Romney and Obama were unable to differentiate the distinctive identity and respective roles of the corporations and the role of owners of corporations in the economic system. Since the views of both of them contribute to the execution of government functions and policymaking, such lack of knowledge or confusion is not good for the performance of the economic system.

If any society accepts the private or even union ownership of means of production and capital, that society also must accept the macroeconomic necessity of the distribution of the distributable income (output) fairly. The private ownership of the means of production should not be a mere instrument or mechanism to allocate the lion's share of distributable income for excessive luxurious consumption of the owners—it must be a useful societal arrangement to ensure economic efficiency. Warren Buffet shows a hint of this kind of understanding.

Policy Question 2
Constitutional Amendment to Have a Balanced Budget

Governments rarely balance budgets. Many Americans think that increasing national debt arising from budget deficits would pose a real threat to the stability of the economy. During the negotiations of the increase of the debt ceiling in 2011, Republican and Democratic representatives of the legislature agreed to a compromise. Part of the compromise requires the House of Representatives and the Senate to vote on a Balanced Budget Amendment to the Constitution, although its passage is not guaranteed. Therefore, bringing a constitutional amendment to enforce the government to balance the budget has become an important policy issue in the US.

The government collects a certain amount of revenue. Also it has a certain amount of expenditures to be incurred, according to the budget approved by the legislature. When the expenditure exceeds the revenue of the government, it is known as having a budget deficit. When there is a deficit, the government has to borrow the balance amount in order to spend. This expenditure is known as deficit spending.

The borrowing limit of the US government is controlled by the BCA (Budget Control Act). Under the BCA, the legislature has the power to increase the borrowing limit or what is known as debt ceiling of the government.

Before the Great Recession of 2008, (the crisis, in fact, began in the summer of 2007), the government's debt in September 2007 was $9,815 trillion.

Subsequent to the economic crash, the government increased deficit financing in order to contain the economic recession; the borrowing limit increased to $14,294 trillion by February 2010.

On May 16, 2011, the Treasury Secretary Timothy Geithner announced that the federal debt had reached its statutory limit and declared a debt issuance suspension period, which would allow certain extraordinary measures to extend the Treasury's borrowing capacity until about August 2, 2011. There was a simple meaning to this announcement, which was if the debt ceiling was not increased on or before August 2, 2011, the government was to default on its monetary obligations.

Then, a bill (H.R. 1954) to raise the debt limit to $16,700 trillion was introduced on May 24 and was defeated in a May 31, 2011, by a House vote of 97 to 318. The House passed the Cut, Cap, and Balance Act of 2011 (H.R. 2560; 234-190 vote) on July 19, 2011. But it did not become a law due to the opposition of the Senate and the incumbent president.

Increasing the debt limit was unpopular. The idea to have a balance federal budget gained momentum. This popular sentiment included in the next bill.

On July 22, the Senate tabled a bill on a 51-46 vote. The measure would have increased the statutory limit on federal debt from $14,294 trillion to $16,700 trillion once a proposal for a constitutional amendment requiring a balanced federal budget was transmitted to the states.

On August 2, 2011, President Obama signed into law a revised compromise measure to raise federal debt limit and that required the House of Representatives and the Senate to vote on a Balanced Budget Amendment to the Constitution, although its passage is not guaranteed. Accordingly, the United States just avoided defaulting of its debt obligations.

This debacle led me to write an article to explain why the constitutional amendment to have a balance budget is dangerous. That article was published in *Asian Tribune* on August 23, 2011.

It is true that the subject of economics has been reduced to a dismal science as we know it today. It is also true that all mainstream economists missed predicting the Great Recession of 2008. Admitting all these weaknesses, *The Economist* wrote, "In other words, economists misread the economy on the way up, misread it on the way down, and now mistake the right way out."

However, when economists fail, politicians want to do everything according to common sense. During the debt ceiling negotiations among congressmen and senators, most lawmakers believed that the government would not face a debt crisis if the government balanced its budget. Even Federal Reserve chairman Ben Bernanke, the top official economist of the country, did not want to go on record rejecting this notion. Finally, as pointed out above, the bill to increase "debt ceiling" was approved on August 1, 2011 with a bipartisan promise to make a constitutional amendment to legally enforce a balanced budget. It looks intelligent, but the opposite is true.

Thereafter, this proposal was getting its power. Politicians, especially Republicans, were—and are—talking about it openly. On a grassroots level, activists worked hard to muster support for the constitutional amendment. I got an e-mail requesting my support. They explained their demands as follows:

American families have balanced their books. And cut spending. It's time for Washington politicians to do the same. Or lose their jobs.

We are demanding two very simple solutions:

1. Demand a balanced budget amendment (70 percent of Americans are in favor).
2. Demand 10 percent across-the-board spending cuts. By cuts, we do *not* mean cuts in the increase in spending. We mean real cuts.

We are working in Washington now to push this common sense approach to legislation. To force this issue, we are gathering the most powerful political force in the America: Conservative Americans 50+.

This proposal was dangerous. I was scared that the demand for a constitutional amendment might get energy because most economists did not analyze the issue critically and express their views openly to the public.

The economy is a system. If you do something in one area, it will affect another area. The proponents of this proposal proudly claim, "American families have balanced their books. And cut spending." The proponents do not understand this is the very reason that Washington politicians can't balance the books of the government. The reverse should happen if the American families want to see that the government balances its books. American families must live beyond their means (increasing spending within borrowable limits) in order for the government to live within its means if the country does not want a recession or economic crisis.

The contemporary economic system is not a balanced system or in natural equilibrium. Commonsense proposals such as those to have a balanced budget would not turn an imbalanced economic system into a balanced one. If economists fail in their jobs, it is not wiser to return to "common sense." On the contrary, we must look beyond the existing paradigm of economists. That is how we can gather new know-how to tackle this kind of economic crises.

There is a fundamental contradiction in the economic system arising at the consumption level due to the system's inability to pay the consumers (so-called American families) an aggregate income that is exceeding or equal to the value of consumables offered by the entrepreneurs in the economic system in the long run. If consumers do not—or cannot—buy what is offered for consumption, entrepreneurs would cut back production.

In the economic system, producers produce two kinds of goods: (1) products for the consumption and (2) products for the use of production (known as investment goods or higher order goods). Therefore, if the production of consumables is cut back, the demand for higher order goods would be reduced and the producers of those goods would cut back on production. This is how recessions occur. This has been clearly explained in Chapter 1.

However, the contradiction or imbalance of the economic system that occurs at the consumption level is temporarily avoided in the short to medium term by a credit mechanism. To put the economic system into equilibrium at a consumption level, consumers need to have extra liquidity beyond their debt-free income so they take loans. If we have this first-level equilibrium, it will lead to equilibrium at total output level. What does this mean? This means consumers (American families) must live beyond their means to be recession free.

If you live beyond your means, you accumulate debts that you can't pay back.

However, if private consumers are supposed to live within their means, two other entities continue to borrow non-repayable debt. Those two entities are the government and the stock and derivatives market. When the government increases deficit spending, that money will end up increasing consumer income, but the government is in debt. The stock market cannot thrive by investing pure savings. If the holders or holding companies of stocks and derivatives continue to borrow to invest, we would have a thriving stock market. When stock prices are moving up, certain income goes for the consumers, but debt is piling up. Chapter 1 pointed out that stock market operations are debt-based processes. When the stock market crashes, those debts become "toxic assets" or bad debts.

The above fundamental contradiction at the consumption level has made the economic system a complex one. When consumers (American families) had huge "bad debt" prior to 2007, we blamed them and those executives who made loans for private consuming families. During the Great Recession of 2008, we blamed speculators of the stock market for the "toxic assets." In 2011, when American families balanced their books and stock markets virtually make no "toxic assets," which would not cripple the banking system, we blame the government for high-deficit spending. Isn't this useless? The truth is that all three entities—private consumers (American families), the stock market, and the government—cannot be "bad debt" free at the same time in the long term.

Apply these phenomena to all countries in Europe and the United States—prior to 2007, during the Great Recession, and thereafter—and you will realize how true it is.

If the system works in that way, by legally enforcing the government to have a balance budget, we remove the government's ability to intervene when necessary. We have to understand the real nature of the contemporary economic system before we put forward any "commonsense" proposals.

It is true—and you may understand that from the theories explained in Part 1 of this book—that continuing deficit financing would not solve the current economic crisis. The real solution we discuss in Chapter 8, but a balanced budget is not the solution or even part of the solution.

Luckily, the demand for the constitutional amendment to balance the budget has subsided. Yet, as I am writing this book, Mitt Romney put forward a catchy slogan. He said he would end the "spending and borrowing inferno." Then he should do one thing. He must ensure that the System Gap is being filled by other two mechanisms—namely private consumer credit mechanism and debt created in the stock and derivative market.

Chapter 8
The Solution

Let us begin from the last paragraph of Chapter 3:

> The System Gap Theory clearly establishes that our economic system is not in natural equilibrium. Evidences show that this disequilibrium is temporarily put into equilibrium by a component of bad debt created in the regime of consumption debt (which includes government's deficit financing too) and in debt created in financial and asset markets. Unfortunately there is no known mechanism to prevent systemic bad debt accumulation which accumulation is proved by System Gap Theory and thereby leaving us with only one solution. That is the beauty of this contradiction because we have only one solution: that solution being the periodic deflation of debt while keeping the "real aggregate consumer" income intact.

Accumulation of non-collectable debt is real. Rex Nutting is MarketWatch's international commentary editor based in Washington. Recently he wrote, "As much as we hear politicians, pundits, tea-party patriots, and the Congressional Budget Office obsessing about government debt, it was excessive private debt—not public debt—that caused the 2008 financial meltdown. And it was private debt—some of it since transferred to the public—that lies behind the current European debt crisis." His observation is accurate.

Why we have enormous amounts of debt?

System Gap Theory establishes that we are trapped in an economic system that requires consuming beyond aggregate consumable income. In other words, the economic system produces certain commodities for consumption, and household disposable income and taxes are not sufficient to distribute the distributable output for the wellbeing of the members of society. The complete distribution of distributable output requires a component of credit. This credit mechanism is not simply to absorb a consumer savings by another consumer; instead, the credit mechanism should be capable of creating more credit out of relatively small incoming cash deposits. To create more credit out of a relatively small incoming deposit or savings, we need the Fractional Reserve Banking system—and we have that in place in our economy already.

Why is it required to consume beyond income? Because we need to ensure that employers would not make a loss in providing employment in producing the given level of output. In other words, such consumption is required to ensure the demand-and-supply equilibrium at consumption level, which leads to achieve the demand-and-supply equilibrium at total output level. In other words, such consumption is necessary to fill the System Gap in order to put the economic system into equilibrium.

A similar gap in the macroeconomic system was observed by Keynes before the conceptualization of System Gap Theory. Therefore, he must have explained the origin of it and a mechanism to resolve the contradiction. Though this has been discussed previously, let us review it here quickly.

Keynes observes that the gap originates due to the increased savings by the consumers as the economy grows. He explains that when the income of community increases, the consumption also increases—but not by so much because as the income increases, people start to save part of the increasing income. So now there will be a gap between the value of output and demand so that employers would make a loss. Keynes says, "The key to our practical problem is to be found in this psychological law" of consumers tending to save increasing amounts as the income increases. This is how the systemic contradiction originates, according to Keynes.

So, he identifies or proposes the solution too. He proposes either we have to increase the propensity to consume or increase investments to ensure that employers would not make a loss at total output level. Increasing investments are also subjected to one important condition. That condition is that we have to increase investments that do not increase the demand for immediate consumption. He said, "Employers would make a loss if the whole of increased employment were to be devoted to satisfying the increased demand for immediate consumption." (Keynes, *General Theory*, p. 27.) In simple terms, what he meant is that current investment should not produce products for the use of consumption immediately but must have demand in the future.

The System Gap Theory rejects both the cause for the origin of contradiction (or gap) and the solution identified by Keynes. The SGT proves that the gap arises due the system's inability to pay consumers an aggregate income that is exceeding or equal to the value of consumables offered by the system. (Since this hypothesis of SGT has been proved in Chapter 3, it is not necessary to discuss it here). This rejects Keynes's "psychological law" of originating the gap.

In Chapter 3, we pointed out clearly that the "conditional investment" mechanism proposed by Keynes is only a mechanism to postpone the current contradiction to a future date. In other words, SGT identifies that even investments (subjected to the above said condition of Keynes) of self-expanded capital and producer credit cannot resolve the systemic contradiction infinitely.

The other proposition of Keynes is to increase propensity to consume. This proposition is based on his assumption that the community saves money as the income grows and which action diminished the demand. If the demand is reduced, employers would make a loss and cannot justify the given amount of employment and the given level of output, so they reduce employment and output, causing a recession. So, he is of the view that if consumers increase consumption as much as the income increased, the system is in equilibrium. But SGT proves that even if consumers spend all their income on consumption, it will not put the system into equilibrium because aggregate consumer income is less than the value of consumption.

Macroeconomic empirical data, prior to the Great Recession of 2008 in the United States and Europe, suggests against the above proposition of Keynes but in favor of the SGT. Before the crash, people had accumulated heavy debt—not savings. So, that private consumer cannot increase consumption. The only option is to increase the consumption of government. That was what Japan has been doing since the early 1990s; by 2012, it has been estimated Japan's public debt would be around 239 percent of GDP. After the Great Recession of 2008, the United States continues to do the same thing; it has been running a $1 trillion budget deficit for four consecutive years. After two lost decades, Japan proved the uselessness of such amounts of deficit spending. No matter how long it continues, continuing deficit spending will not bring the system's equilibrium.

The United States temporarily stopped the recession by incurring heavy deficit financing. But the system is not in sustainable equilibrium yet—even by 2012. If we cut back deficit spending, the economic equilibriums will break, which would put the system back into a recession. Even though Keynesianism was recalled to resolve the Great Recession of 2008, their approach proved disastrous, by mid-2012, the US national debt surpassed well over 100 percent of GDP.

Keynes's "psychological law" may be valid for an individual household, but evidence suggests that on a macro (national) level, that does not hold. Keynesianism was unable to identify the root cause of systemic debt crises. Obviously, the Keynesian solution must fail due to its inability to understand the root cause of the crisis.

Keynes should be respected for identifying a systemic contradiction that needed to be fixed. As far as I know, monetarist school of economics, Austrian School of economics, or any other school of mainstream economics did not identify the said systemic contradiction or the gap in the macroeconomic system. For example, Austrian School sees the problem in the Fractional Reserve Banking system and wants to end the Fractional Reserve System along with Central Banks. Monetarists see the problem in loose money and "big government."

A careful observer (I can't remember his name) said the difference between monetarists and Keynesians are about 3 percent. This means if monetarists want a higher rate of interest for their tight money policy (5 percent interest), then Keynesians want to have 2 percent interest for their loose money policy (the difference is 3 percent). Also if monetarists want 3 percent deficit spending (as mentioned in the European Union Monetary Stability Pact), Keynesians prefer to increase it to 6 percent when necessary (again the difference is 3 percent). This might be the reason that the said economist observed that the difference between Keynesians and monetarists is just 3 percent.

Even though this might be true when it comes to economic policy application, Keynes clearly identifies a systemic contradiction—but none of the other schools of economic thought failed to do so.

The modern economic theories and algorithms are dismal failures in analyzing the macro system. The failure of the hypotheses such as Efficient Market Hypothesis (EMH), Rational Expectation Hypothesis (REH), and Dynamic Stochastic General Economic Equilibrium (DSGEE) arise from the fact that the proponents assume that economic system is in natural equilibrium. System Gap Theory explains that the economic system is not in natural equilibrium. Therefore, when the equilibrium cannot sustain the current level of output, those hypotheses fail. SGT further explains that in certain periods the economy grows due to a few unsustainable mechanisms filling the economic System Gap. These mechanisms are unsustainable because they create an unsustainable amount of bad debt in the system in three specific areas: (1) private consumer regime, (2) the government, and (3) stock and derivative markets—or all three areas.

Hyman Minsky identifies the accumulation of bad debt in the economic system and presented his Financial Instability Hypothesis (FIH). Minsky identifies hedge, speculative, and Ponzi finance as distinct income-debt relations for economic units; debt on hedge financing as stable while debt on speculative financing and Ponzi financing are not stable. He asserts that if hedge financing dominates, then the economy may well be an equilibrium-seeking and containing system: conversely, the greater the weight of speculative and Ponzi finance, the greater the likelihood that the economy is a "deviation-amplifying" system. Thus, the FIH suggests that over periods of prolonged prosperity, capitalist economies tend to move from a financial structure dominated by hedge finance (stable) to a structure that increasingly emphasizes speculative and Ponzi finance (unstable).

To explain the hypothesis, Minsky defines hedge, speculative, and Ponzi financing as shown below:

- For hedge finance, income flows are expected to meet financial obligations in every period, including both the principal and the interest on loans.
- For speculative finance, a firm must roll over debt because income flows are expected to only cover interest costs. None of the principal is paid off.
- For Ponzi finance, expected income flows will not even cover interest cost, so the firm must borrow more or sell off assets simply to service its debt. The hope is that either the market value of assets or income will rise enough to pay off interest and principal.

When speculative finance and Ponzi finance grow larger, the economy takes on much risky credit. Now it is only a question of time before some big firm actually defaults. Lenders understand the actual risks in the economy and stop giving credit so easily. Refinancing becomes impossible for many, and more firms default. If no new money comes into the economy to allow the refinancing process, a real economic crisis begins. (http://cambridgeforecast.wordpress.com/2010/04/13/minsky-concept-of-ponzi-finance-and-galbraith-concept-of-the-bezzle-financial-crises/

Most of the speculative and Ponzi debt became bad debt. According to Minsky, that is how system accumulates bad debt.

> In short, Minsky emphasizes two propositions: 'that the internal workings of a capitalist economy generate financial relations that are conducive to instability and that the price and asset-value relations that will trigger a

financial crisis in a fragile financial structure are normal functioning events." (Ingham G., *The Nature of Money*, p. 161.)

Minsky identifies the accumulation of bad debt (instability) in the system and says that such events are normal functioning events. He proposes a solution. "From a Minskian perspective, the avoidance of crises by expert monetary and financial management is merely a postponement. If debts are not expunged through bankruptcies, they remain as an 'overhang' that might be triggered into a chain of defaults." (Ingham G., *The Nature of Money*, p. 162.)

So, the solution is to cancel uncollectable debt or bad debt.

System Gap Theory is contrary to the Minskian perspective. SGT explains that after a period of economic growth, if the private consumers are not in significant debt, then the government should be. And if both the private consumer and the government are not in debt significantly, then the System Gap must be filling from the income derived from the stock and derivative market, which means there should be a bubble in the stock market with heavy debt on holders or holding companies of stocks and derivatives. If nothing of above is happening, then it must be an immature economy that is expanding by reinvesting the expanded capital and producer credit, mostly producing goods and services that do not satisfy the demand of immediate consumption. In all former scenarios except the last scenario, the economic system should crash sooner than later if partial debt cancellation does not take place proactively. In the latter case, the economy would fall into any one of the former scenarios as the economy grows. The only other possibility that a producer country does not have a "debt" crisis is that it continues to have excessive (I mean excessive) trade surplus; but all countries in the world cannot record "excessive trade surpluses."

Accordingly, Minsky identifies only the crisis of one of the three debt centers in the economic system: the bad debt in stock and derivative markets. After a crisis, consumer credit and credit to stock and derivative market usually diminish. As a result, the government tends to run high deficits but it is not a solution as we have already seen from the Japanese example.

In principle the solution proposed by SGT is very similar to Minskian proposal; the solution is the "expunge of bad debt."

But if the system's instability arises from speculative and Ponzi financing as pointed out by Minsky, the best thing is to contain the speculative and Ponzi financing. That is common sense. In order to contain the speculative and Ponzi financing, we need only a simple reform in the monetary policy.

We can stop credit financing of stock and derivative purchases by designated commercial banks. As a result of this reform, the commercial banks would not fail when speculative or Ponzi financing failed. And also this policy would minimize the speculative and Ponzi financing because now the banks deal with limited resources (without credit money of commercial banks) in financing stock purchases. The commercial banks are the banks that could create "credit-money" in the economic system under the Fractional Reserve Banking system. Therefore, when the creation of new "credit-money" to finance stock purchases is prevented, debt-based speculative activities will be minimal.

But Minsky did not propose it. Instead of stopping debt-based speculative and Ponzi financing, he suggested to "expunge debt through bankruptcies" to go for another cycle of the same. Does this mean that he observes that accumulation of bad debt is unavoidable in the normal functioning in capitalism? In regard to financial markets, the answer must be yes—but what's the situation in the regime of consumption? Should they be allowed to accumulate bad debt and be expunged? There is no answer to this question in the Minskian theory.

However, if we wish to stop credit financing of stocks and derivatives by commercial banks, the implementation of this rule must be through an international convention in order to put all countries on an even playing field.

Perhaps after this rule is implemented, there won't be much bad debt accumulated by speculative and Ponzi financing that requires to be "expunged." So, the implementation of this rule is strongly advocated by SGT. But that is not enough. Why?

When we contain speculative activities, naturally that will reduce the income that could be allocated for the use of consumption. So, we need to increase the debt level of private consumers or the government—or both. But this increase will be a fraction of debt that the debt requires to increase if the speculative and Ponzi financing is tolerated. In Part 1 of this book, it has been pointed out that stock and derivative market operations are not purely based on savings, but much of it is debt-based. Further, it has been pointed out that in order to fill the System Gap, it is required to create more credit in the stock and derivative markets than is required if the credit flows directly to consumers.

As a result, when we need to expunge bad debt from the system, we expunge consumer bad debt—and not the bad debt of speculators and Ponzi financiers.

Cancellation of bad debt is a bad term. One might think that it would lead to a moral hazard because people might take excessive loans, expecting cancellation. This happens if debt cancellation takes place on a case-by-case basis by allowing bankruptcies. That is what Minsky had proposed in regard to speculative bad debt in the financial market.

In fact, this was what exactly happened in America, Europe, and China immediately after the great crash of 2008. Bailout packages were designed by governments and Central Banks to save crashing capitalist enterprises—and much of it went to the financial industry to save banks, mortgage lenders, and insurance houses. Since the government increased deficit financing, some called it a return to Keynesianism. Some Keynesian economists pointed out that Keynesianism is not about pouring public money into bankrupt private enterprises. That is why they call it "bastard Keynesianism." In reality, what had been implemented until early 2010 was not Keynesianism—it was Minskianism. Subsequently, up to now, Keynesianism is in effect—but already Minskianism and Keynesianism have failed. The reason is that none of it is capable of removing systemic bad debt out of the system.

SGT establishes that periodic debt cancellation (a more sanitized term is debt deflation) is a systemic requirement to ensure the continuing equilibrium of the economic system. This is a theoretically verifiable proposition. It cannot be empirically verified until the cancellation is effected through some kind of policy.

Once you accept the need for cancellation of the part of uncollectable debt, it is common sense that it requires inventing new macroeconomic policy tools for the cancellation of systemic bad debt.

So, how do we cancel the part of uncollectable debt in the system with containing or without containing the speculative and Ponzi financing?

The best way is the deflation of debt through wage increase bound moderate inflation. In other words, we increase the minimum wage by a suitable percentage. That will cause a positive inflation that helps to cancellation of the part of debt. In other words, this will reduce the debt-to-income ratio of consumers and would cancel the part of government's cumulative debt in real terms. According to SGT, we can't increase wages to put the system into equilibrium, so the objective of increasing wages is to activate a secondary mechanism that puts the system into equilibrium.

In a recent study published in the US, it was reported that if the minimum wage is increased by 70 percent to $12.30 per hour from $7.25 per hour, inflation would be 3 percent. Maybe the estimates would not be accurate to the exact point, but it reveals the correlation of minimum wage increase and inflation.

But there is a strong opposition to increasing wages—especially during a recession. They suggest that it will increase business cost and lead to further layoffs. The truth is far from this assumption.

As we know from the Mechanics of Recessions, during a recession there are employers who have losses due to a lack of demand. The demand-and-supply equilibrium is necessary to end the crisis. Also we know from SGT that this equilibrium is met only with a component of consumer credit, which includes private consumer credit and the government's deficit spending.

If we continually increase deficit spending, we have a bigger government and use more resources for the "out-of-market production." This will reduce the economic efficiency. (We explained this point in Chapter 4). That is not what we want. We want an efficient economic system, which is possible only with a large enterprise base and a smaller government. Therefore, there is only one option left: reviving the private consumer credit mechanism. This we can't do if we can't reduce the current consumer debt-to-income ratio. This is where wage increase bound moderate inflation is useful. That will effectively reduce the debt-to-income ratio, which will induce consumers to borrow and lenders to lend. In other words, the consumer credit mechanism is revived.

When the consumer credit mechanism is revived, along with new consumer credit and household income, it brings along the demand-and-supply equilibrium. At a macroeconomic level, employers would not make a loss—even if the government's deficit spending is reduced. The businesses should be made to understand this macroeconomic behavior to enable them to make adjustments consciously and willingly. Therefore, the whole objective of minimum wage increase bound moderate inflation is to ensure that employers would not make a loss due to continuing depressed demand.

However, if there are businesses that are temporarily vulnerable to minimum wage increases, the government can extend temporary taxation remissions. This will be a much lower cost for the government because the government is not required to increase deficit spending to fill the System Gap—and the government's revenue increases due to proportional increment of payroll and other taxes.

Therefore, the argument that minimum wage increases might lead to cut jobs by entrepreneurs is kindergarten economics. From the System Gap Theory, we have no illusion that we can't put the economic system into equilibrium by increasing wages. Instead, wage increases might partly cancel old debt and since consumer can have access for new credit and that will increase consumer liquidity (income plus credit) in order to ensure that producer entrepreneurs get back what they expect from consumers. When this happens, we have the supply-and-demand equilibrium at consumption level—and that will ensure the equilibrium at total output level. Increased wages will increase moderate inflation, but now the consumers have the means to buy them. That is what entrepreneurs want. The macroeconomic objective to increase wages in an economic recession helps the producer and entrepreneur more than it hurts them.

Also, the government can increase the stock of base money, which is debt free on the government; but government can't do this if the dollars in circulation are going to increase more than the necessary amounts. But we can stabilize the total money in circulation if we increase the MRR (mandatory reserve ratio) stipulated for commercial banks while increasing the stock of base money. If the response of increasing MRR is long term then the Central Banks can introduce SLR (Statutory Liquidity Ratio) as a monetary policy tool. The total money in circulation is a function of these two variables (stock of base money and the stock of credit money created by commercial banks). That is why we can use the policy in difficult times.

This policy does not suggest converting the banking system into a Full Reserve Banking system. Because if we increase the MRR to 100 percent, the banking system will be a Full Reserve Banking system, removing the power of creation of credit money by commercial banks. SGT completely rejects the proposition of implementing Full Reserve Banking system and proved that the macroeconomic fundamentals demand the Fractional Reserve Banking system. (Please refer to Chapters 1 and 3.)

The contradiction that we have in our economic system is systemic and requires a systemic solution. The minimum wage increase bound moderate inflation is a systemic solution. Is there any moral hazard in this strategy? No.

In a systemic crisis such as this one, the best deflation of debt could be done through wage increase bound moderate inflation. From the perspective of creditor nations, this is a crime because wage increase bound inflation reduces the real value of their dollar—or euro-based assets. That's the price they have to pay for continuing trade surpluses. Europe paid this price when the US unilaterally jettisoned the Bretton Woods Agreement in 1971. But the world moved on.

The said solution is applicable to Japan even after two lost decades. Increasing deficit financing cannot keep Japan afloat. Japan's public debt is expected to reach 239 percent of GDP by the end of 2012. This cannot go on infinitely. Many in Japan say, "We see no alternative."

The alternative is the use of System Gap Theory to resolve systemic non-repayable debt.

Chapter 9
The Question of Pension Planning

In the introduction of this book, I mentioned that I need to treat the subject of pension planning as a macroeconomic subject. First let me explain why I want to do that.

Some mainstream economists agree in regard to the ongoing global economic crisis that when everything fails, we have to resort to the inflationary solution. Can we judge whether every known solution would fail beforehand? That is important to prevent people suffering job losses and businesses suffering income fears. Every time there is an economic crisis, we do not need to inflate the system. That is why we need to recognize which crisis is needed to be resolved through wage increase bound moderate inflation and which is not.

Certain debt crises are different from others. Surely the economic crisis that triggered in late 2007 in the US and in Europe was different from the previous crises. To explain the difference as far back as 2008, I wrote, "This was a different kind of crisis and invented the term 'terminal recession' to define it. I used the term terminal recession to define that beyond a certain point of economic growth, the economy cannot remain as it is or grow any further without canceling a good part of consumer debt." (*Indispensable Bad Debt*, 2008). If I replace the word "recession" for the word "crisis," the observation would have been well versed as the governments have temporarily halted the recession with excessive deficit financing.

Many mainstream economists—even four years after the eruption of the crisis—still did not come to this understanding. They still bet on Minskianism and Keynesianism.

Therefore, what the economists should do is recognize which crisis is a terminal crisis and which is not. In a terminal crisis, we will end the previous debt cycle by general deflation of debt in order to begin a new dynamic credit cycle.

Therefore, as part of the solution moderate inflation is a must. (Please refer to Chapter 8.) At inflation, one of the first groups of "victims" would be retirees. They should not suffer at an old age—as they are—because they cannot be too sure of a better tomorrow. We must secure their livelihood. That is the very reason I need to treat this subject of pension planning as a macroeconomic subject.

Any efficient pension reform must reduce the present burden on workers and employers and offer more benefits—not vice versa.

Let us look at this issue from a macroeconomic perspective to formulate a reasonable reform bill. Usually economic theory gives us more clarity to put new policies and programs in place.

The first economic truth in regard to an efficient pension scheme is that "you can't save for your retirement—instead you pay for the pension of retirees of today and your retirement benefit will be paid in turn by future generations of the work force."

Under this principle, two important parameters are automatically adjusted in calculating the present-day retiree benefits in the process of economic evolution; those are (1) adjustment for inflation (2) adjustment for ever-increasing productivity. These two adjustments do not happen in "save-for-your-pension" programs.

The notion that you can save for your retirement—and by investing those savings "wisely" you can have a rich retiree life—is a big illusion. The proponents of this idea usually say, "Let the pension savings come to the financial market, and the market will grow." They benefit the investors (i.e. prospective retirees). This illusion came to a virtual end after evaporating the pension savings with the Great Crash of 2008 in the United States.

Why does society need a pension scheme? Let me explain it.

At any given time, the economic system produces two kinds of products: (1) products for consumption and (2) products for the use of production (i.e. capital goods).

Products for the use of consumption are needed to be distributed among the members of the society. Part of it should go to retirees. According to the economic principles, total revenue in the country is generated by the current workers—and not retirees. So, what is supposed to be distributed for consumption, in fact, should be distributed among the current employees—and they are supposed to take care of their elders. But this does not happen to the satisfaction of elders or to the satisfaction of present employees. The solution is to allocate part of the distributable income to senior citizens by a mandate. The mechanism for such an allocation of consumables and distribution of it among senior citizens is popularly known as pension; this is why we need pension programs.

How do we allocate part of the consumable income of the system to seniors? The only way to do is to collect a "tax" from current employees to pay for today's retirees. It is a welfare tax paid by all employees of today to pay for the senior citizens of today. Current employees will get it back in the future when they retire. When this "tax" is related to a percentage of earned income of present employees, they will have their benefits in the future automatically adjusted for any possible inflation—and for increases of productivity too.

By any means, a pension is a "tax" on current employees that requires distributing part of the present consumable output as deemed fit by social norms. We can make this "tax" appear to be as a saving of the payee, but it cannot be a saving. Because the fundamental economic truth is that the economic system can't pay a higher aggregate income to consumers than the value of consumption. Therefore, what is allocated for consumption by way of salaries and wages must be used for consumption. Therefore, you have to use the income for your consumption or to pay somebody else's consumption to put the economic system into equilibrium. This means macro-economically beneficial and efficient pension schemes are those where inflow equals outflow.

The concept behind pension funds is a myth. You can't build up a pension fund if inflow equals outflow at any given time period. There should be a surplus to build a fund. It is an excessive saving. Such excessive saving from consumable income breaks an important equilibrium in the economic system because consumers spend lower amounts for buying consumables, which is bad for the producer/entrepreneur. This means the demand-and-supply equilibrium breaks at the consumption level with excessive savings; if that happens, economic equilibrium at a total output level breaks, leading to an economic crisis or partly aborting potential output.

Also if your retirement benefit is not guaranteed, you try to save more for your retirement. Assume that your retirement is guaranteed with an inflation-adjusted retiree income—you are more comfortable using consumable income for the use of consumption. This means you do your obligation to ensure an economic equilibrium as a consumer by spending your income after paying a "retiree welfare tax/saving" which is used by another person for his consumption in real time.

As pointed out above, excessive saving out of consumable income—whether it is voluntary or compulsory—is bad for the economy. This can be prevented by having a secured pension program. Therefore the need for a good pension program is a macroeconomic necessity—as well as a social obligation.

So, now the economic theory behind pension programs is clear. Accordingly, we will have the most efficient pension program when the inflow equals outflow in real time.

If we design the pension scheme according to the "inflow equals outflow" principle, we can bring down the current percentage of contribution toward pension funds while guaranteeing more benefits to the retirees. On the other hand, such reductions in paying toward pension schemes will relieve employers and employees.

Also there is a popular myth arising from the political left. They think pension programs should not be "contributory" from the worker. Let us analyze this matter quickly. Pension allocations should come from the "consumption money" allocated in the system. Consumption money belongs to households—not to enterprises. If an enterprise pays the contribution of pension of an employee, it is just an accounting adjustment—and such payment duly must be posted under the cost of wages and salaries. Therefore, pension contributions are always coming out of workers; there is no other way to do it.

Let everybody contribute to somebody's pension today and, in turn, the retiree benefit of the present contributor will be paid in the future by future generations in the workforce. This is the kind of pension reform we need today. It will be a national pension program. This kind of pension program will be beneficial to employers, workers, retirees, producers, entrepreneurs, and the whole economy. This does not mean that individuals are banned from saving or investing more for the future—whenever and wherever they want—but it should not be an alternative.

A universal pension fund will guarantee a fear-free retirement to all. Retirees do not want to fear inflationary effects—and they benefit when productivity increases even if they are retired. The government will have little trouble administering it. There will be no corruption—or corruption will be minimal—as there are no long-term surpluses in the pension program. Pension funds should not be a source to boost the stock market or for the government to borrow.

Chapter 10
Conclusive Remarks

Many economists believe that aggregate consumer income (i.e. disposable income + taxes) is just sufficient to consume the consumable output. Within this system, credit is simply treated as absorption of somebody's savings by another. But the System Gap Theory has proven that, in order to consume the consumable output in the medium to long term, we need the disposable income plus taxes plus a component of non-repayable debt (bad debt). Even some economists realize that loanable funds could be more than savings (this means credit is not simply absorption of somebody's savings by another) under the practice of Fractional Reserve System, they never hypothesize that the system has to create a component of bad debt to ensure the system's equilibrium.

So the above said component of bad debt should keep on accumulating during periods of economic growth in three specific areas, namely (1) in private consumer debt regime, (2) in the debt regime of stock and derivative markets, and (3) in national (public) debt regime.

If the provision (or creation) of bad debt is stopped because of the busting of a debt bubble, the producer employers should make a loss leading to reduced production; such reduction of output for two consecutive quarters is defined as a recession.

Such recessions, or crises triggered because of bad debt, are severe systemic crises. Also systemic crises are different from other crises due to the fact that those crises can be resolved only by the removal of a good part of non-collectable debt; and for this reason, such crises can be named as "terminal economic crises" or "terminal recessions."

Accordingly, the Great Recession of 2008 is a terminal crisis because, in order to find a lasting solution to the crisis, it was and is required to remove a large amount of non-collectable debt.

Unfortunately there is no known mechanism to remove enormous volumes of bad debt from the system. Expert monetary management by the Federal Reserve of the United States and its counterpart, Central Banks in other countries, might achieve temporary consolation, and most of the time such consolation would not last for long.

In a terminal economic crisis, usually austerity measures do more harm than good because such measures do not ensure that employers will not make a loss at current and increasing output levels. You would witness this folly of Europe firsthand before long; however, a creative central banker along with the government would find out that the best systemic debt deflation could be accomplished through minimum wage increase bound moderate inflation; implementation procedures are just details. This policy action would not hurt producer entrepreneurs, as it would ensure that employers would not make a loss at increasing total output levels; and this is the first condition that requires ending the crisis. The Federal Reserve's expert monetary policy management, which is typified by quantitative easing and by keeping the rates low, could only be complimentary to the implementation of the said policy. This policy would help to reduce governments' borrowing without any negative impact on economic recovery. That's the only path to quick and sustainable recovery of the current global economic crisis. "We hate inflation, but amazingly this is a situation where (minimum wage increase bound) moderate inflation can save us or the world" (*Indispensable Bad Debt*, 2008, p. 49).

Finally, in view of the above, we need to redefine the subject of macroeconomics. Macroeconomics is not just about full employment and inflation; instead, it is about maintaining the demand-and-supply equilibrium at increasing total output levels, facilitating full employment and low inflation during normal periods of growth, and moderately inflating the system to deflate debt from time to time when it is necessary. Periodic deflation of debt is an unavoidable necessity of the economic system under the present practice of Fractional Reserve

Banking system, because we cannot prevent bad debt accumulation while ensuring growth; bankruptcy laws, however extensive they are, are not sufficient to do it. That is why a systemic solution is needed. In other words macroeconomics is about filling the Economic System Gap; Central Banking and macroeconomic policy management should focus to achieve this goal.

Paradigm Shift and Kalama Sutta

Thomas Kuhn (1922-1996) was an American philosopher and a historian of science who coined the term "paradigm shift." Some argue that he did not coin the term. But whenever I want to refer to the term, it is always linked to Professor Kuhn. I prefer to use how he defined this term.

> A scientific revolution occurs when scientists encounter anomalies that cannot be explained by the universally accepted paradigm within which scientific progress has thereto been made. The paradigm is not simply the current theory, but the entire worldview in which it exists, and all of the implications which come with it.

Even though Kuhn used the term for science, it is now commonly used in other disciplines to explain when there is a change in fundamental assumptions in current views requiring a paradigm shift. This is what is necessary now in macroeconomics. But this progressive change cannot take place if your mindset is not right. What kind of mindset do we need for a paradigm shift? Just read below the oldest suggestion (about 2,600 years ago) I could find in regard to having the right mindset to make a paradigm shift.

> Do not believe in anything (simply) because you have heard of it.
>
> Do not believe in any tradition because they have been handed down for many generations.
>
> Do not believe in anything because it is spoken or rumored by many.

Do not believe in anything (simply) because it is found in your (religious) books.

Do not believe in anything merely on the authority of your teachers and elders.

But after observation and analysis, when you find that anything agrees with reason and is conducive to the good and benefit of one and all then accept it and live up to it.

—Kalama Sutta, The Buddha

References

Blinder, S. Alan, "Central Banking in Theory and Practice," MIT Press, 1998.

Conrad, Edward, "Unintended Consequences," Penguin, 2012.

David, Kumar, "Essays on the Global Economic Crisis," The Ecumenical Institute for Study and Dialogue, 2010.

Freidman, Milton and Schwartz, Anna Jacobson, "A Monetary History of the United States 1867-1960," Princeton University Press, 1993.

Ingham, Geoffrey, "The Nature of Money," Polity Press, 2004.

Keynes, John May Maynard, "The General Theory of Employment, Interest and Money," First Harbinger Edition, 1964.

Lucas, E. Robert, "Rational Expectation and Econometric Practice," University Minnesota Press, 1984.

Marx, Karl, "Capital," www.marxists.org/archive.

Marx, Karl, "Critique of the Gotha Program," www.marxists.org/archive.

Paul, Ron, "End the Fed," Grand Central Publishing, 2010.

Podoloski, T.M., "Socialist Banking and Monetary Control," Cambridge University Press, 1973.

Poole, William, "Money and the Economy: A Monetarist View," 1978.

Rothbard, Murray N., "America's Great Depression," Fifth Edition, The Ludwig von Misses Institute.

Senanayake, Hema, "Indispensable Bad Debt," AuthorHouse, 2008.

Stiglitz, E. Joseph, "Free Fall: America, Free Markets, And The Sinking of The World Economy," W.W. Norton & Company, 2010.

Trotsky, Leon, "The Revolution Betrayed," www.marxists.org/archive.

Weintraub, Sidney, "Capitalism's Inflation and Unemployment Crisis," Addison Wesley Publishing Company, Inc, 1978.